Intermittent

Bliss

Reflections on a Long Love Affair

by Willem Lange

University Press of New England

HANOVER AND LONDON

University Press of New England

37 Lafayette Street, Lebanon, NH 03755

© 2003 by Willem Lange

Printed in the United States of America

5   4   3   2   1

LIBRARY OF CONGRESS CATALOGING-IN-PUBLICATION DATA

Lange, Willem, 1935–
   Intermittent bliss : reflections on a long love affair / Willem Lange.
     p. cm.
   ISBN 1–58465–304–3 (pbk. : alk. paper)
   1. Lange, Willem, 1935– 2. Lange, Ida. 3. Essayists—United States—Biography. 4. Married people—United States—Biography. 5. Man-woman relationships—United States. I. Title.
CT275.L2723 A3   2003
973.9'092'2—dc21   2003003863

Most of the stories in this collection have appeared in edited form in *The Valley News*, Lebanon, New Hampshire. Some of them have also been aired by the author on Vermont Public Radio as part of his weekly commentary series.

This book is lovingly dedicated

to the young people who pledge

to cleave to each other till the end of their lives

without any appreciation at all

of how long, how short, and how precious life is.

Two are better than one . . .
for if they fall, the one will lift up his fellow,
But woe to him that is alone when he falleth . . .

If two lie together, then they have heat.
But how can one be warm alone?

—*Ecclesiastes 4:9*

Contents

CONTENTS

Introduction

It was after dark. My friends and I had just passed
successfully through United States Customs at
Derby Line, Vermont. We crowded the seats of a big
van, with a great pile of luggage in the back, reeking
of wood smoke and damp neglect. We'd been away
from home, canoeing in northern Canada, for three
weeks. Our minds were still a thousand miles north,
in a vastness without trees or people or darkness. But
all of us were married, and each in his own way and
to his own extent was looking forward to seeing his
wife again. Our driver, a woman, had come from
home to pick us up at the airport and had brought
her fifteen-year-old daughter along for company.

We were all tired and not looking forward very
cheerfully to picking up our lives again the next
morning. The conversation was desultory, muted,
and pretty much restricted to people sitting side by
side. Nobody had the energy to raise his voice for a
larger audience for very long. But at some point
somebody must have said something about marriage, because suddenly it became the topic of a general conversation and clearly had engaged everyone's
attention. There must have been a comment or
truism offered about the value—maybe even the
necessity—of the commitment required to hold a

marriage together, because the teenager remarked that she failed to understand what was so important about that.

When you're young, she said, you don't have experience, and you're likely to make a mistake in choosing a life partner. Then there's all the trouble and fuss afterward of dissolving the relationship. Just look at the statistics on divorce. Far better to live together for long enough to know what you're doing, and then either decide to get married or go your separate ways.

Now, that's an argument none of us heard very much when we were young, during the years of the Eisenhower presidency. Much less would we ever have heard it made by a fifteen-year-old. Those were the days when divorce, when it occurred, was mildly scandalous, and our mothers cautioned us against playing with the children of single parents. So, sitting in the van, I kept my ears cocked for the reactions of my friends. To my delight, none of them broke into a homily, or quoted Goethe on commitment, or even waggled a cautionary finger. Most of us, rather, seemed to mutter something that sounded like "Uh-huh," and to exude a vague, faint disapproval of a point of view with which we had all dealt personally, in both our own lives and those of our kids. The air was pregnant with thoughts keeping their own counsel. When you've been married about forty years, as all of our group had—or over the course of forty years married more than once—it's hard to preach the standard party line with a straight face.

My own opinion is that marriage is largely oversold and virtually always misrepresented by those of us intimately involved with it. Almost every parent or marriage counselor I've ever known has uttered ad nauseam the standard boilerplate: "Marriage isn't all fun and games, you know. It takes a lot of hard work!" I suggest the people who say that suffer from poor imaginations, have seriously limited vocabularies, or have never done any really hard work. It's like warning someone about to swim the English Channel: "You know, you may get a little damp."

Tolstoy—who had a fiercely combative and mutually destructive marriage—comments in *The Kreutzer Sonata* on the illusion of the idyllic honeymoon. It's like a man, he says, suckered into a sideshow that advertises a bearded woman and a water-dog, only to discover nothing more exotic than a bearded man in a dress and a dog wrapped in a walrus skin swimming in a bathtub. Emerging deeply chagrined, he is encouraged by the barker to tell those outside how much he liked the show. Unwilling to disillusion anyone, he endorses it heartily.

Then there are those among us who claim that marriage is a sacred and immutable institution. That to me better describes the New York Stock Exchange, the Vatican, or Harvard University. Marriage, for all its biblical justifications, is about as sacred as sausage, and more an organism than an institution: one as delicate, diaphanous, adaptable, basic, and tough as a jellyfish. There are times at which, in order to stay the course, you have to believe that your marriage—or something or someone, at least—will change. That exercise, and its results, help to develop some perspective.

Every so often we're confronted by the interview

with an elderly couple who've been married an incredible number of years. Like centenarians, they're invariably asked the same type of stupid question: To what do you attribute the success of your marriage? And invariably they give an answer just as dumb as the question; something like: We just always respected each other's opinions, or we went into separate rooms to cool off if we disagreed, or we both said we were sorry. Oh, yeah? What about the time she wanted the house painted yellow or not at all, and he adamantly wanted white? Or when her chilblains were aching and she wanted to sell the house and move south, and he wanted to stay where you could at least tell one season from another? It's easy, long after your fires have been banked, to look back and chuckle at the heat you generated in the past. But at the time of those disagreements, somebody had to give in.

Which is the whole point of it. You learn to give, to compromise, to accommodate. Only people who can do that can avoid snapping in a storm.

We need someone to disagree with us, to take an opposing point of view, to tell us now and then that an idea we have is a crazy idea, before we begin to think it makes sense. We need a little conflict to keep us sharp and sane. A spouse—usually our complement in almost every way—is uniquely qualified and positioned to supply that: to say, "That's nuts!" before we actually are nuts. People like Ted Kaczynski, Timothy McVeigh, and David Berkowitz didn't have that check on their imaginations, and in isolation they began to believe and act out their fantasies.

A lot of us need each other in order to become our best selves.

The question, of course, is whether a roommate or significant other can do it. My answer is maybe, but I doubt it. Living together without both names on the deed, or without the benefit of laws governing communal property, or with the knowledge that you can walk away from it anytime, is like playing poker for matches. It's fun, but it doesn't teach you as much about yourself or your friends as does playing for cash. Far better to ante more than you can afford to lose, play the hand you're dealt, and let it ride. Like democracy, it's not perfect; but it's a long, long way ahead of whatever's second best.

Courtship
&
Marriage

The One Irresistible Woman

It's been said that for each man there's one irresistible woman. I hope that's true; and if there's more than one, I don't want to know about it. I've got all I can handle right here.

This story starts in July 1959—or rather, because of July 1959. Syracuse, New York. Corner of State and Fayette. It was just after lunch, and it was hot! The boss and the state inspector had disappeared together into a nearby tavern. The equipment operator, leaning against his roaring air compressor, hollered to us half-naked laborers and pointed to the bank down the street, where the big clock / thermometer read 106 degrees at 1:06.

Down in our hole beneath the pavement it was even hotter. My buddy Al and I were running a jackhammer, breaking up the walls of an old underground concrete chamber and tossing the debris up onto the street. When we climbed out to take a water break now and then, 106 degrees felt almost refreshing. Al was pretty black, and I'm pretty white; but by quitting time most days we were both the color of concrete dust.

It wasn't a bad job, though. Union wages, $2.47 an hour. The men were almost all really good workers, and the boss one of the best I've ever worked for. We were enlarging and reinforcing old manholes for new electric and telephone cables. Right beside our construction site rose the bulk of the telephone company building, where the operators, during the hottest summer months, worked split shifts. This meant twice the usual opportunity for girl-watching—which, in the days of the Eisenhower administration, is what it was still called.

There were some very nice-looking young ladies in the twice-daily parade. We whistled at them all, and each of us had his particular favorites. But not one of them, after a brief initial inspection, ever gave us a second glance. That was all right; we weren't expecting them to. Shirtless most of the time, and smeared with mud and dust from the excavation, we were not a very attractive group of men.

But then one day, out of a clear blue sky—the thunderbolt! She had short, curly black hair and a pink complexion; sunglasses like Audrey Hepburn, sneakers, and a black dress; graceful of carriage and mighty of figure. I was stunned, captivated. I gaped and whistled. She turned for one heartbeat, looked, and then continued on her entrancing way with her chin just a little higher in the air than before. "My god, Al!" I said. "Did you see that?" Yes, he had; but she wasn't part of his universe, and he couldn't be personally interested. He grinned sympathetically and rolled his eyes.

I had to see her again! But Al and I had dug the hole down to about ten feet deep; we could hear the street all right, but could see it only now and then during breaks. We were throwing our excavated dirt up onto the pavement above, where there was a kid whose job was to shovel it away so it wouldn't fall back down on our heads. I paid him two bits a day to let me know when he saw her coming. He'd stage-whisper down into the hole, "Here she come, man! Here she come!" I'd climb up the lattice of reinforcing rods so that my head was just above street level and watch her go by. Once or twice I whistled, but she never turned her head again. I was in an agony of frustration. I had to meet her somehow. But whistling was obviously no way to do it.

We had a truck driver on the job, a college boy, who spotted me watching her go by one day. "Hey!" he said, "I think I know her! I think she went to Central High when I was there."

"What's her name?"

"I don't know. Ida, I think, and she's got kind of a funny last name. But I remember her. I think she's kind of . . . uh . . . different."

Perfect! Just my type, and the first break in the case, as well. So the next time my lookout up top alerted me to her approach, I climbed up and hollered, "Hey, Ida!"

She stopped and looked for the person who'd called. She saw who it was, turned, and continued down the street. I couldn't take it anymore. I climbed out of the hole—a vision in denim, sweat, and mud—and trotted after her. I caught her at the mailbox as she stopped to mail a letter.

"Excuse me," I called, and when she turned: "Excuse me. Didn't you go to Central? I think my sister knows you."

I don't know where ideas like that come from. Desperation . . . or Providence, maybe. It wasn't planned to do anything but stop her for a second. Which it did.

"What's her name?" she asked, in a voice like velvet bells.

"Diana Lange."

"What sorority was she in?"

"Err . . . Philomathean, I think."

Another stroke of pure luck. She'd been in the same sorority and couldn't remember my sister, which I later found was a major gaffe. It put her on the defensive. But I didn't know that. I plowed onward.

"I just wanted to apologize for whistling and everything when you go by," I said. We don't mean anything rude by it. I mean, we're not all lowlifes down there. Some of us are college boys, and it kind of hurts our feelings when people think we're just a bunch of bums. Maybe you could wave or something now and then when you go by. I won't whistle; I'll just wave hello. Okay?"

The college-boy bit struck pay dirt. Yes, she said, she would. We parted, she resumed her walk, and I went back to the hole in the street.

"Well?" asked Butch Beattie. "What'd she say?"

"I told her some of us were college boys, and she said she'd wave from now on when she goes by. But I am gonna get a date with her tonight!"

"Oh, yeah? What's her name?"

"Jesus! I forgot to ask. But I'll tell you what. I don't know how, but she and I will be at the Velasko Inn tonight at nine o'clock."

"Like hell you will."

"Okay, here's a bet. If we're there, each of you guys

owes me a beer. If we're not, I owe each of you a beer. How's that?" That was fine.

I left work at four o'clock, all in a stew. How could I find her? I called my sister, who gave me the names of all her girlfriends who worked at the phone company. I got out the phone book and started down the list. Everybody knew something, but no more than I did already. Then the last one—Cindy Naulton, God bless her!—said, "Oh, yes! Her name's Ida something-or-other, and she's living at the YW. But they won't call her to the phone unless you know her last name."

This was progress, but I was stymied without a last name. Still, nothing venture, nothing win. So I called the Y and asked for Ida. "Ida?" said the desk girl. "Ida who?"

"Oh . . . gosh!" I said, "wait a second. I have it right here." I crumpled a piece of paper next to the receiver and made frustrated sounds. "Uhh . . . I know I have it here . . . "

"Do you mean Ida Capron?" she asked. I wonder now, over forty years later, whether the desk girl could have had any inkling how deeply she would affect several entire lives with that one question.

"Yes, yes! That's it!" I mean, how many Idas could there be?

"One moment, please." She rang the extension.

"Yesss?" It was her! With the voice like velvet bells and a rising inflection that I've come to recognize over the years as that of someone always ready for something new.

"Hi," I said. "This is the guy from the pit."

"Who is it?"

7

"You know: the guy in the hole in the street. I spoke to you today, remember?"

"Oh, yes . . . "—a pause—"Could you hold on for just a minute."

"Uhh . . . sure." Did I have a choice? I heard the clunk of the receiver of a pay phone being put down upon a metal shelf. Then fading footsteps and silence. Shit! But I waited anyway. I'd come too far, and the prize was too great to quit now.

Three minutes later I heard the phone being picked up. "Yes?" she asked.

"I was just wondering if you . . . if you'd like to go out sometime and have a cup of coffee downtown or something. You know, just talk."

"Sure," she said. "When?"

"Tonight?"

"Sure. What time?"

"About eight o'clock?"

"Okay. I'll see you then. Come in and ask for me at the desk."

I pulled up in front of the YWCA two minutes before the hour, gave my hair a lick and a promise, and went in. She appeared about thirty seconds after the desk girl called her, which meant she'd been ready, too. I don't know what she was expecting when we stepped outside, but what she got was a brand-new Beetle convertible with a German shepherd puppy in the front seat. "This is Hans," I told her. "I didn't want to leave him home." She'd decided while getting ready that it wasn't safe to go anywhere with me in a car because she had no idea who I was. But when she saw the puppy, she changed her mind. She got in and pulled Hans into her lap as if it were the most natural thing in the world to do. And off we went to the Velasko Inn.

Who knows what we talked about? It was a sizing-up session, and from where I sat, everything was just the right size. She wore a light blue acrylic sweater with a scoop neckline like Marilyn Monroe. Holy Toledo! By nine o'clock I had completely forgotten we were expecting guests. But they came leering in, like a troupe of baboons, right on the button: Butch and a couple other guys. "Hey, Will! How's it goin'? Whatta ya doin' here? Who's your friend?"— stupid stuff like that. She looked a little panicked, and I was definitely telling them with my eyebrows to beat it, so after joining us briefly in the booth, they did.

A little later we drove down to Onondaga Park and took a walk. At the park's most romantic spot, the lakeshore under the weeping willows by the arched bridge—street lamps across the lake reflected in the water—I recited "The Love Song of J. Alfred Prufrock" and some other equally inappropriate poetry.

It was, as they say, a successful evening. I didn't know it, but the reason she'd put down the phone when I called was that she was asking her roommate to take her date that evening. She'd been sure I was going to ask her out. Nor did I know that, while I was droning my way though "the cups, the marmalade, the tea, among the porcelain . . . " down in the park, she was being charmed by what she later called "the soul of a poet." Yes! The Poet in the Pit!

We parted late that evening with a clear intention to continue. And we did, too—every night, just about, for the next six weeks of the summer. I traded the Volkswagen for a roaring old Jaguar roadster, in which the three of us (remember Hans?) cut quite a swath. Then in September she went back to college in Virginia, and the whole thing began to look like a summer romance. I stayed on at the construction job, which was slowly winding down. We wrote letters back and forth now and then, but nothing much seemed to be happening.

Then one afternoon, as my psychiatrist and I (that's another story) were sort of summing things up at the end of the hour, I said, "You know, I often wonder why I didn't ask that girl this summer to marry me. It seemed like a perfect match."

"Well, why don't you?" he asked. So that night I called her and did. She thought I was telephoning under the influence and asked me to call back in the morning. In the morning she said yes. We were married just about twelve weeks after the day she walked past the manhole.

That's the beginning of the story.

Sliced Virginia Tomatoes

IDA WAS GOING TO SCHOOL AT A SMALL women's college in Harrisonburg, Virginia, a town that advertised itself as "The Turkey Capital of the World." Good title. She was living not far from the campus with a family named the Petersons. In exchange for her room and board, she baby-sat the two kids now and then and helped out on the family egg farm. The family spoke in standard third-generation American Southern accents but had hung on to their Northern European fascination with regularity; their poor kids got dosed with a laxative every night before bed. Considering Ida's cash-strapped situation, though, and her long experience with kids, it beat paying for a dorm room.

She was virtually independent of her parents, who a few years earlier had separated after years of acrimony, abuse, and midnight calls for the police. She didn't know where her father was and didn't want to know, except to keep an eye out for him; he was forever popping out of nowhere with ominous phone calls to the family she lived with. She knew where her mother and sisters were, but was only now and then in contact—mostly because the sisters had a knack for spilling information to the old man whenever he emerged unexpectedly. So there were none of the usual problems with parental approval. I met her mother and sisters at the wedding reception and her father about five years later.

My family, on the other hand, was quite well organized, but in its subtle way as much a burden to me as hers was to her. We planned to marry in Harrisonburg in late October. We were both Episcopalians, so my father the Episcopal priest would, of course, do the blessing of the marriage at the conclusion of the ceremony. But thanks to his airtight schedule, the only day he had available to do the job was Saturday, October 31—and he had to be home in Syracuse in time to get to his services the next day.

We were young and practically indigent. Anything anybody else did for us felt like a tremendous favor. The ladies of Grace Episcopal, for example, mindful of Ida's virtual orphancy, offered to decorate the church and throw us a reception—a truly lovely gift. On the other hand, it never occurred to me that a father would pass up a couple of church services to marry his son properly. Apparently, it didn't occur to my father, either. So Halloween it was, and to save gas, we'd drive down and back together in Dad's '58 Chevy—my parents; a strange, fey, bearded friend of mine named Deacon who'd agreed to usher; and I— and then back Saturday night with the addition of my bride and her foot locker.

I'll tell you, if the old man tried to pull that sort of thing on me today, I'd offer my regrets and find another priest. Not only would I refuse to let us be squeezed in, but Halloween is a lousy day to get married. For years afterward, you have to take your kids trick-or-treating. After they grow out of that, you have to stay home to receive other kids coming to your house. Now that finally we live on a remote road in the woods and nobody comes to the door anymore and we're free to go out, we go out—and everybody's in drag! The holiday seems to have become the night for folks of other persuasions to come out and cavort. Mother and I, dressed for a romantic, formal dinner out, feel a little funny surrounded by strobe lights, loud music, ecstatic screams, and Bengal tigers and warlocks locked in amorous embraces. Take my advice: Never, never get married on Halloween! I don't care if your father's the pope.

The four of us started south long before dawn Friday and arrived in Harrisonburg in time for lunch. We met the cautious, polite Petersons. We exchanged painful pleasantries (which is always more difficult for people startled by my father's collar and sign-language-only deafness). I was long accustomed to Yankees, who don't talk a lot but imply a great deal by what little they say, or even by what they don't say. Suddenly I was surrounded by people who talked a lot, but didn't seem to mean anything by it. If there were implications—and I was pretty sure there were—I was missing them: "Hah, how yew doin'? So nahss to see you! This you fowtha? How yew do, Rev'nd?" There was an undertone, and it wasn't pleasant.

Finally we escaped for the evening and, when my best man and another usher showed up from North Carolina in an old Opel, to a fluorescent-lighted diner for a mild bachelor party.

Meanwhile, after taking one look at me Friday at lunch, the lady of the house, Melza Peterson, offered

Ida the keys to the family car, just in case she changed her mind about the next day. She implied pretty heavily that anyone in her right mind would certainly change it.

Ida told me about it, which would have surprised Melza, for discreet Southern ladies keep such secret maneuvers to and among themselves. But she did tell me, and it kind of set me crossways a little. But at lunchtime Saturday—not a jolly event—I rallied and asked if I could help get it ready. I decided I could be nice for at least a couple of hours, especially considering the prize at the end.

"Wha yes, you can hep," said the lady who I now knew had offered my intended her car keys. "You can cut up these tomatoes and put 'em on this plate." I rinsed off the tomatoes, picked up a knife, and went right to it.

"Here, here!" she cried, when she saw me at work. "First you have to peel 'em! They've been layin' against the dirty old ground. Always peel 'em! That's the way we do it here in the South."

"Well, by god," I answered, "this is the way we do it in the North! Just like potatoes; skin's the best part of 'em." And I went right on slicing, skins and all. Dirty old ground, my foot!

I thought, if only I can just get through the next few hours without tangling with this lady, we're out of here, and I'll never see this town again. So I kept my pinky high as I sipped my tea at lunch, and noticed that Mrs. P. didn't eat any tomatoes. I murmured appropriate pleasantries and prayed that when it came to the point in the service at which the minister asks if anybody has any objections, she'd hold her peace.

Which she did. But there was a moment of anxiety as my bride and I faced the priests and a sudden flurry of activity disturbed the silence behind us. It was loud enough to make us turn around. But it was just my mother-in-law-to-be, arriving late, noisily shushing three of her young daughters and wearing a black dress as she made her way to a front pew. I didn't know much then, but I began to sense, in a rudimentary way, why my beloved had distanced herself from her family.

We returned to the Petersons' after the ceremony and reception, to change for the long drive back to New York State that night. My father was in a stew to get going. My bride headed upstairs to her room; I picked up my overnight bag and started up after her.

"Here, here!" cried Madame Defarge (she was really into that here-here stuff). "Where do you think you're goin'?"

"Upstairs to change."

"Wha, that's unheard of!" She pointed to the study. "You get back down here and change in there. Wha, you Yankees! I never . . ." The way she said the word, "Yankees," I could picture a horde of soldiers in blue, poised at the Pennsylvania border to rush South again, raping, pillaging, and burning. I yearned briefly to be one of them.

But again I kept my peace, and shortly after dark we were off on our journey. Those were the days before the interstate highways, and U.S. Route 11 took us through a hundred small towns on its long way north. In every one, little ghosts and goblins with shopping bags prowled the sidewalks, traveling from house to house in search of goodies. Jack-o'-

lanterns glowed beside porch steps, and long gar-
lands of toilet paper hung from tree branches above
the road. It was a surrealistic start to what has been
an unbelievable experience. Yet there's been very little about it I'd wish to change. And I'm still damned
if I'll peel tomatoes!

The Honeymoon

OUR HONEYMOON, SUCH AS IT WAS, lasted about twelve hours. We pulled into my parents' driveway in Syracuse just about dawn on Sunday morning. My father splashed his face, put on a fresh collar, and headed off to Rome for a couple of services that day. Deac lay down on the living room couch, covered himself with newspapers, and fell asleep, with his long, scraggly beard hanging down across the Saturday headlines. My mother told us we could sleep in the master bedroom. Then she put on her coat and disappeared. That was the start of the honeymoon.

The two of us were pretty tired, but not exhausted. Still, the novelty of our wedding rings and unexpected situation—not to mention that of licit love— proved somewhat distracting. It was also frankly weird to be lying in my parents' bed and in their bedroom: the seat of rectitude, as it were. The specter of the rest of our utterly unplanned lives loomed at the foot of the bed, looking remarkably like my father. We knew that I had to go to work again the next morning; that I would be laid off soon; and that we had a temporary billet with my folks. Beyond that, nothing. What a marvelous thing it was to be young and able to subsist on little more than hope!

Sometime during the morning Deac got up, stole quietly out of the house, and caught a cross-town bus back to his place. Left alone together at last, we lay in bed looking at old family photographs. There was a lot we didn't know about each other or our respective families yet. The pictures began to color in the sketch.

Suddenly there was a loud, confident knocking at the front door, downstairs. I pulled on a pair of jeans and went to answer it.

A robust elderly lady stood on the porch, poised to knock again. She wore a cloth coat and carried a shopping bag. I opened the storm door. She walked in without being asked.

"Are you Reverend Lange?" she asked.

"No, he's away till tomorrow, but I—"

"I'm here from the Trinity Church Every-Member Canvass. Have you had a chance to pledge yet this year?"

"Well, no. Actually, I don't go there—"

"Let me give you a pledge form, then." This woman was not to be deflected by even fairly obvious signals.

"Okay, that's fine. I'm not going to fill it out right now. I just got married yesterday, and my wife and I are resting . . . "

"Oh, that's nice. Is your wife an Episcopalian?"

"Yes. We both went to Trinity when we were younger."

"Was your wife in Girls' Friendly Society?"

"Uh, I don't know." I hollered up the stairs: "Honey? Were you in Girls' Friendly?"

A strangely strangled voice from the second floor: "Yes . . ."

"Did you know Sue Morse?" the old gal shouted. I couldn't believe this conversation!

"No, I don't think so."

"Excuse me," I said. "I'll go up and put on a shirt." I bounded upstairs, made a few weird faces at my bride to tell her there was a nut in the hall, and grabbed a T-shirt. Suddenly we heard firm footsteps coming up the stairs. I dashed to the top and stopped her on the second landing. While I held her there at bay, she and Ida carried on a surreal conversation, whose substance I don't recall, across the length of the upstairs hall. Finally I ushered her firmly back to the front door and out onto the porch. I waved my pledge card gratefully at her as she turned to leave and stomped off to her car.

My mother came home that evening, and that was the end of the honeymoon. Next morning I went back to work at the construction site. That evening, after a day of scrubbing concrete forms, I came home to supper for the first of what would be thousands of times. All very ordinary and prosaic. But if I'd had my wits about me in those days, I'd have realized that with a bizarre start like that, our life together was going to be a wild ride. I'd have been right, too.

Across the Threshold

As expected, I got laid off the construction job just before Christmas. The boss had been very kind, knowing I'd just gotten married, and had kept me on long after my buddies had gone off to the unemployment office. But the number of dirty concrete forms at the yard was finite; eventually I had all of them scrubbed, oiled, and ready for spring.

Unemployment insurance has always been anathema to me; it takes a little of the edge off motivation. I answered want ads till I got a job driving night-shift taxicab in Syracuse. Ida found a spot clerking in an S&H Green Stamp redemption center. So we were both working, at least; but we now got to see each other less than two hours a day, as we passed on the way in and out. Thus, when I considered that my professional dealings were all with people of the night —drunks, whores, felons, news reporters, and guilty husbands—and further, that my net take averaged thirty-five cents an hour, I could see that a change was necessary.

I called my old boss at the Lake Placid Bobsled Run, where I'd worked the previous couple of winters as a laborer and, when the run was operating, public address announcer. "Where the hell have you been?" he shouted into the phone. "God, I've been hoping you'd call!" Those words are among the sweetest an unemployed working man can hear. So a couple of days after Christmas the two of us piled virtually everything we owned into or onto the Jaguar roadster and drove through lowering skies and high snow banks to my old ten-dollar-a-month apartment in the Adirondacks.

She'd been there before during the summer, but this winter situation was new to her. The apartment was on the second floor, accessible by a flight of open stairs on the outside of the building. The eaves above the stairs dripped, and formed a line of ice right down the middle of the treads; anybody climbing them looked from behind like the back end of a bear with its legs wide apart. Carrying her up the stairs was out of the question. But once we were assembled at the top, I kicked open the door and carried her across the threshold . . .

Into an icebox. It was colder—or at least seemed to be—inside than out. So I set Ida down, looking somewhat forlorn, in the middle of the room and hustled back down the stairs for a gallon of kerosene from the barrel under the stairs. I showed her how to start the fuel flow into the pot burner and touch it off with a piece of flaming toilet paper. The water pipes weren't frozen because of the heated apartment downstairs (of which more later), so I showed her how to start the propane gas hot water heater in the kitchen. Then I started ferrying our stuff up the stairs for her to put away in the dresser, or hang on the wall, or stow on the kitchen shelves.

"Will!" she cried a few minutes later. "The ceiling is dripping!" And so it was. The ceiling was finished with four-by-four-foot square sheets of beaverboard, with lath tacked over the joints. For some time, apparently, the flat tin roof above the ceiling had been leaking into the space between. The water had frozen in large, flat sheets, also about four feet square, that lay in the slight concavity of each square of ceiling board. I could hear them jiggle and bump when I pushed up on the beaverboard. Now, as the room warmed, they were sweating rusty water through each sheet in half a dozen places apiece. It was my first practical homeowner's test as a married man. I took decisive action.

Down under the stairs I had about a dozen old sap buckets I'd used the previous spring in a kitchen-stove sugaring operation. I brought them up and set them in the sink to thaw the ice off them. I took a lead pencil and poked a hole right in the sagging center of each piece of beaverboard and set a bucket under the resulting stream. Later, when the dripping had stopped, I taped a little X of masking tape to the floor to mark each bucket's location. Then, after every heavy rain or snow, or when we went away overnight, we always put the buckets on the marks.

There were other little domestic tricks she had to learn. The piece of lath in the kitchen was to prop shut the oven door, which was slightly sprung. The hot water heater took about half an hour to heat enough water for a bath. Only the right-hand kerosene drum under the stairs was ours. Most important, our septic system was a fifty-five-gallon drum buried in the back yard. We shared it with the LeClair family of five downstairs, and it was in a constant state of overflow. Foozie LeClair, the mother and alpha member of the pack, had three kids in diapers but no washing machine; so she washed the diapers in the kitchen sink and rinsed them in the tub. It was critical, I informed my bride, with heavy emphasis on the adjective "critical," never to flush our toilet when we knew Foozie was rinsing diapers. This would overload the plumbing, pop the stopper out of Foozie's tub, and take her right back to square one, as it were.

I haven't the words to do justice to Foozie. When agitated by events in our apartment above her, she often ran out into the road in front, shook her fist up at our porch, and yowled a stream of imprecations that, as the Victorian explorers used to say, can be better imagined than described. This lovely-looking little woman could string together a series of oaths and epithets that, if you were to read it, would make no sense. But somehow, when she performed it, it assumed a symphonic quality. I could only marvel at her talent. Naturally, my bride forgot about not flushing during the rinsing below, and I came home from work one day to find her in tears, cowering in the corner of the bedroom. "You can't imagine . . . " she said, sobbing. "You can't imagine what she said!" Actually, I could. And I knew the light of my life would never forget again.

At the end of my first day at the bobsled run, I drove home in the gathering darkness for the momentous occasion of our first supper together in our first home. I parked the car in the snowbank out front, filled the kerosene can she'd left on the stairs for me, and climbed to the second floor.

I walked in the door and sniffed. "Mmm," I said.

"What's that? Chicken?"

"Oh! No, I haven't started supper yet."

"Well, that's okay. I'll take a bath while you do."

"Oh, dear! I haven't started the water heater, either."

It was, as I had hoped it would be, a momentous occasion. I prayed it wasn't portentous, as well—a prayer that has been answered.

Our apartment had a floor of unfinished maple. While I was at work one day, my wife scrubbed it. The soapy water must have changed color when she got to the duffel-bag-size dark stain in the middle of the living-room floor. When I came home, she asked me what it was.

"Oh, that's just blood," I said. "I got a buck last fall and hung it on the pole over at the saloon for a couple of days. But then I had to go away for the weekend, so I brought it over here and left it inside. I guess it wasn't quite drained. Made quite a mess, eh?"

I could see she believed it was blood, all right; but from the way she looked at me, I think she was seeing Bluebeard. She scrubbed that floor about once a week from then on, and after a while that spot was even brighter than the rest of the floor.

When we'd left Syracuse, we'd brought with us, besides everything we owned, all the money we had, which was very little. The job at the bobsled run paid well, but there was a three-week hold on the first paycheck. Luckily, my mother had given us as a going-away present a case of canned baked beans and a case of stale hamburger buns. That was it for three weeks. At lunchtime at work, the old-timers straddled the sawhorses nearest the stove and opened their lunch pails to discover egg salad or ham salad sandwiches wrapped in waxed paper; Thermoses of hot, sweet coffee and steaming soup; dill pickles also wrapped neatly in waxed paper; and covered plastic bowls of tapioca or butterscotch pudding. I opened mine to a hamburger bun as dry as an old egg carton filled with government-surplus baked beans. In my Thermos was either cold water or, on a good day, hot tea with government-surplus dry milk to thicken it up. God knows what my wife was eating at home. We were expecting a baby already, so I hoped it was something decent.

My first paycheck finally came. The boss liked to dress up in his state trooper outfit—jodhpurs, big fur-trimmed coat, and sealskin hat—and hand out the checks to all of us in the shop at quitting time, along with a warning that anybody who spent his check on the way home and as a result didn't show up the next day was fired. I carried mine straight home, cashed it at the grocery store, and gave my wife her weekly allowance for food—eight bucks.

It was a very long season. Jaguar roadsters aren't designed for commuting—much less starting—in Adirondack winters. Once I got to work, though, I enjoyed it. It was often arduous and sometimes boring, but I've always loved working in gangs of men, especially when there are old-timers in the crew. When the run was operating, I stood in a glass booth opposite the snack bar and announced over the public address system the progress of each sled as it came down the mountain.

Back at the apartment, however, there must have been very little stimulation for her: a new woman in a very small and self-contained village; no television or record player, an old tube radio that got the CBC in Montreal and little else; and a few books. Looking back, I don't see how she did it. When I came home about dark, I typically bathed, ate, and passed out till five the next morning. Occasionally I mustered the consciousness for a game of Scrabble. We've saved our best scores for over forty years now.

Marriage was something we'd both planned on since childhood, and tough times weren't strange. We planned on staying married to each other for the rest of our lives. But, if we'd appreciated then what was ahead of us, and how long a life really is, and that life inevitably ends with an unhappy event that everyone tries to avoid—I can't finish that sentence; I don't know what either of us would have done.

We lived then on energy, habit, and hope. It was wonderful to be young and strong, able to run and dance, and to think of life as infinite. All of those facts and illusions are gone now. But I don't think I'd repeat those days if some playful fate gave me the chance. Once across the threshold is enough.

Family

The Baggage We Bring from Home

Therefore shall a man leave his father and his mother, and shall cleave unto his wife: and they shall be one flesh. That's what the Torah says (translated into sixteenth-century English), and it may be true. But in the leaving and cleaving we carry and bring with us far more than we suspect and often more than most of us are willing to admit. It's a large part of who we are. We never get rid of it or, I suspect, completely outgrow it.

When my wife and I clove, I don't think that either of us at all suspected how much baggage we were bringing to the union. She came to me with a purse and one footlocker, her name painted on the lid, and literally all her earthly belongings inside. Lying flat at the bottom were three twelve-inch LPs: *Moonlight Sonata, Die Moldau,* and a recording of the young Princess Elizabeth and her baby sister, Margaret, assuring the children of Great Britain that they were with them in London, in spite of the Blitz. I had a few more things than she, but we were able to move our possessions in one trip with the roadster. We were not much troubled by earthly baggage—except, perhaps, the damned roadster—but we were almost overburdened by the loads in our heads and hearts.

I knew that her family had had some problems, that she'd left home at sixteen, had pretty much raised her younger sisters, was already a terrific cook, and had been living on her own for the three years before I had met her. She knew that I came from a stable, religious home, was in remission from a college career, had (as they say nowadays) some anger-management problems, wrote poetry, and was gainfully employed as a construction laborer. That's all we knew about each other. But at the time that was enough. We were in a chemical state.

This evening, as I write this up in my office, I can hear her making little noises in the kitchen at the foot of the stairs. It sounds as though she's putting a salad together. The kitchen TV is playing softly. I can envision the scene perfectly. It's so tranquil and ordinary, it's hard to imagine the stresses and pain that first drove her away from her home and later made us irresistible to each other. To this day, nearly half a century later, I don't approach her from behind without speaking, or stand still beside her bed while she's sleeping. We share our life with a specter.

She was the oldest by seven years of five daughters; a sixth had died in infancy. She remembers those first seven years as happy. Her parents were among the heirs to a disintegrating fortune and in those days still had hopes. Those hopes had begun to wither shortly after the second child was born, and the marriage had begun to disintegrate in argument, frustration, and violence.

"I remember when I was ten," she told me sadly one day. "Patty was three, and my parents were separated. They had a big fight and she got a court order to keep him away. But he used to come late at night and cut the phone lines and then break in. So my mother told me, if he broke in again and began to beat her up, I should go next door to the neighbors' and call the police. Well, my bedroom was right next to where the phone lines ran down the side of the house, and you know how light I sleep. I slept even lighter in those days.

"One night I heard the phone lines make that noise they make when you cut them. Then he smashed in the front door and began to beat her up down near the bottom of the stairs. So I slipped past them, went next door, and woke up the neighbors. It was like two o'clock in the morning! I said, 'I need to use your phone.' Here was a ten-year-old kid at two in the morning asking to use the phone! I think they called the police for me.

"The cops came and stopped the fight. I was standing on the porch when they brought him out. He saw me and stopped, and he said, 'I'll never forgive you for this! Never!' Then I had to go to court and testify, while he sat there glaring at me. He got ninety days in jail, and when he got out, they got back together again. That's when Susie was conceived. So there they were, all reconciled, and there I was, a little kid all by myself, just waiting for him to get even with me."

He was a construction engineer, which is a traveling occupation, anyway; but for one reason or another, he couldn't keep a job, so they moved dozens of times. The money ran out, the abuse resumed. They sold the house that was a gift from her mother, sold the furniture, and began renting—usually till the rent came due. They moved to Toronto, Buffalo, Labrador, Rome. There were times the kids were in orphanages. One of the most poignant stories my wife tells is of being put into an orphanage in Utica and separated from her sister Patty. She missed her terribly, so one day she just walked out and began searching the city for the other orphanage.

The best times for the sisters—five of them now—were Saturdays, when they spent the day at the movies, and Sundays, when they could spend most of the day at church. "I'm sure most of the people at church knew why we were there, but it was never mentioned. We had something to eat after church and hung out in the Sunday School rooms, coloring and telling stories. It was a lot better than going home. Those weekends were when I really learned to be creative with baby-sitting." The Episcopal Church —often of gray stones with a red door—has ever since been a symbol of strength and charity for her. She's utterly devoted to it. Sometimes priests mistake her zeal for a reaction to their personal or professional qualities. It's not that. It's the institution.

By the time she was fifteen, the abuse had become not only more physical, but less predictable. Relying on intuition—which she retains and trusts implicitly to this day—wasn't enough to keep her out of harm's way anymore. And she was no longer a child; she began to see beyond baby-sitting and refereeing family battles. So when her injuries put her into the hospital for the second time, she confided in a sympathetic priest. She asked him to help her find a private school that would take a kid with no money but a lot of needs.

The first choice, Northfield School for Girls, wouldn't take her unless she repeated her junior year. That, she said, I'm not going to do. I want to get away as soon as I can. Next the priest found a tiny, struggling Episcopal school in the mountains of Virginia. The Blue Ridge School was run, appropriately, by an old priest named Father Loving. When she asked Father Loving if she could graduate in six months, he said, "Well, yes, we can take a look at where you are, and perhaps give you some extra assignments, and I shouldn't be surprised if you could."

She could, and did. She remembers the last few weeks of school, just before graduation, when the school's food money ran out. Signs in Virginia vernacular—NO 2NDS OWN AIGS—began appearing on the cafeteria counter. The seniors voted to forgo meat and vegetables so the little kids could have them, and for the last week they dined ceremoniously on bread soaked in milk and sugared.

"That school was the turning point of my life," she says. "I thought I had it pretty hard—and I did—but those poor little kids from the mountains . . . Every Sunday they'd get washed up and dressed in their best clothes. Then after chapel and lunch they'd sit around the flagpole waiting for their parents to show up. And lots of times they didn't come. The kids'd say something like, 'Oh, they're late this week, but I know they're a-comin.' And just before supper they'd say, 'Well, I guess my mama couldn't get a car this week, or maybe papa's sick again . . . '

"It just broke my heart to see them like that, you

know. A few didn't have families at all, and they were spared the disappointment. But I never heard a word of criticism of the parents that didn't show up. That was the first time I ever saw kids worse off than I was, and I thought, 'Thank God! In another couple of months I'm out of here, and I'm going to work. That awful stuff is behind me, and I'm going to make it!'"

During the summer, Father Loving called her. In one last demonstration of the devotion found in the hearts of only the very finest teachers, he'd rooted around till he'd found a college scholarship designated for young women like her. Was she interested?

That college today is James Madison University; back then it was Madison College, a small Virginia girls' institution dedicated to the education and protection of young Southern women of modest means. She didn't have the money to join a sorority, and she didn't have a mother able to send the school a list of the young men approved for dates. So she didn't date; she worked. Victorian values and the honor code hung like the sword of Damocles over every impulse. She was almost expelled for stashing a possum under her bed and failing to report herself.

Summers, she returned to Syracuse, where she had a few roots, and worked as an operator at the telephone company. By the summer of 1959 she'd finished three years of college, but the unremitting discipline had begun to tarnish the goal somewhat. "I was tired of school and working two jobs all winter. I was tired of being alone and feeling inferior to the other girls at school. And the thought of going back to live with the Petersons was almost more than I could face. They wanted to adopt me and never really got over it when I said no. I didn't need any more complications. My father was driving me crazy. He'd found where I was, and he kept calling the school and the Petersons. He even had me pulled out of an exam one day for an emergency. All he wanted was for me to get hold of my mother and try to 'talk some sense into her.' I'd had it!"

And then one day that summer she walked past a manhole where there was a young man working who was also pretty sick of being alone and found her irresistible.

I've often wondered: Do other people get married because they can't help it, or do they just grow into the idea and decide, yeah, this seems like the natural thing to do? For us—in retrospect, at least—it was an ineluctable thing and had nothing to do with common sense. Both of us were wound so tight and so dissatisfied with our states that marriage was a release rather than a logical or intelligent thing to do. And I had baggage, too.

My future wife's family was so wildly and clearly dysfunctional that it's pretty easy to trace her habits and inclinations, her affections and aversions back to their origins. Mine wasn't so easy to figure out. It was, to all outward appearances, pretty serene. A friend once asked me, "When you think of your childhood, what one word best characterizes it?"

"Security," I answered. I didn't even have to think about it. Shadowed by three living generations of ancestors, I hadn't an anxiety in the world. Great-Gramma Lange was my nanny; Grampa and Gramma Lange ran a sedate and mildly successful pharmacy on the ground floor of our four-story apartment building; my father had a job, in spite of the Depression; and every morning I got a penny to spend any way I wished. I'm sure there were hard times for my parents—there might even have been some days when they wondered if they had enough to make it to the next paycheck—but I was never aware of it. My parents were deaf, but we communicated in sign language, something I never knew wasn't normal till I was older and my friends told me. The family was conservative, Republican, and evangelical. All of them thought I was the greatest kid in the world and saw their job as keeping my feet upon the straight and narrow biblical path, avoiding the abyss on either side. I suppose I would have found that onerous eventually, if it had lasted.

But for years my father, who was working as a meat cutter at a local packing plant, had been attending church services for the deaf at a nearby Episcopal church. He read well, so he'd become a lay reader. Then the aging priest, about to retire, persuaded him to study for the priesthood at home. He studied nights at a big oak desk just on the other side of our bedroom wall. In February of 1943—I was almost eight—he was ordained and took over a mission to the deaf that stretched over four dioceses, from Albany to Buffalo and from Poughkeepsie to Malone. That summer, in order to be closer to the center of his mission field, he moved our family to Syracuse.

The change was cataclysmic for me: from a fourth-floor flat a couple of blocks from the state capitol to a shingled bungalow with lawns front and rear, a driveway, and a garage. But also from the warm, protective cocoon of an extended family to an alien existence in a neighborhood of Irish Catholic kids who found my vocabulary and pronunciation strange, my spectacles laughable, and my parents weird. My sister and I fit in all right, eventually—she better than I, thanks to a bosom buddy—but the big change for me was the loss of my father.

That's not a complaint or a whine; it's just a fact. He was gone a lot of the time, especially on weekends. For a while he traveled by bus and train, using his clergyman's certificates for fare discounts. It was the middle of the war, and there were no automobiles being built. But in 1945 he was able to get a 1942 Chevy, which made his travels a lot easier. I'll give him this: He came home as often as he could, sometimes driving heroically through the late evenings or storms to make it. The sound of his car in the driveway past midnight and the front door closing after him are as comforting to me in memory as they were then. But his attention and his passion were focused elsewhere.

It's ironic that the church that provided with one hand such a haven for a young girl and her gaggle of sisters took away with the other hand a young boy's father. It made her an enthusiastic lifelong supporter of the institution and me a dour lifelong critic. It left her grateful and me angry. The church paid my father very poorly for the incredible effort it took to cover that huge field for over forty years, and the penuriousness trickled down. He received four cents a mile for his travel, from which he paid in turn for the car itself, and gas and oil and repairs. He kept meticulous records—I've always felt he missed a calling to bookkeeping—and, incredibly, he was able to save enough in the Car Fund to trade every two or three years for a new car.

This was the only household fund that ever had more than a few dollars in it; everything else was budgeted monthly at anticipated expense. As I approached the threshold of adolescence, I often needed more money than my allowance provided. So I would occasionally ask to borrow from the Car Fund. It was a humiliating experience: "This fund is for the Lord's work, so when you borrow from it, you are borrowing from the Lord." Even at that age, I could think of good arguments against that buncombe, but I always needed the money more than I needed my pride.

My future wife and I had moved in some of the same circles, shared some friends, and even attended the same church when we lived in Syracuse. But she's almost five years younger than I, so as kids we never met. Quite coincidentally, each of us in our fifteenth year reached the crisis that changed the courses of our lives and brought us to conjunction at the corner of State and Fayette in 1959.

The crises occurred, of course, five years apart: hers in 1955, when she left home and started at Blue Ridge, and mine in 1950, when I was judged a juvenile delinquent destined for Attica or Sing Sing and was sent instead to the Mount Hermon School in Massachusetts. As Blue Ridge did for her, so did Mount Hermon change my life. That may be a cliché, but it's true in my case. The baggage was still there—especially the anger at abandonment—but the regular schedule and discipline (which I never tested) were just what I needed at the time.

What I didn't fully appreciate then was that, even though the school's tuition was only $750 a year, and they gave me a $400 scholarship, we still didn't have an extra $350 to pay the difference. So my mother went to work as a stock clerk at a local department store. It probably was good for her to get out of that lonely, unstimulating house, and that a good friend of hers, also deaf, worked with her. But when I think now of her riding the bus downtown and pasting price tags onto dry goods for eight hours every day in that windowless basement, I'm mortified to remember I never thanked her. It's possible, according to some of the faithful, that I may someday be able to. But I doubt it, so instead I do what I can nowadays to help other kids in the same pickle.

Three years at Mount Hermon may have saved me from further trouble with the law, but they left me totally unprepared for the freedom of college life. There followed five years of wandering: in and out of the College of Wooster in Ohio, and a year at Syracuse University. I spent a winter living in Greenwich Village, working for a midtown publisher. Hitchhiking through northern Ohio one winter night, I was in a wreck that should have killed all of us in the car, but somehow didn't. I signed up for ROTC, disliked military discipline, dropped out, and got drafted. But the injuries from the car wreck had made me 4-F, much to my delight. I moved to the Adirondacks, rented the apartment to which I would eventually bring my bride, and landed the job at the bobsled run. I was working, but I was a mess; my parents must have been going nuts. Then in the spring of 1959 I got the construction job that brought me to that street corner in Syracuse.

A few months later my bride and I pooled our resources and began to make a life together. We also pooled our baggage, which didn't seem a very important thing at the time. I've learned since that it's our baggage, at least as much as our resources, that determines much of the nature and quality of a life.

You Can't Choose Your Family

IT HAD BEEN A DISASTROUS WEEKEND so far. I had ignored an important self-imposed rule and broken polite protocol. I had agreed to travel on Labor Day weekend, finally met more than half a dozen of my wife's relatives in one pack, and offered to take one of the most obnoxious outside.

It's true: You can choose your friends, but you can't choose your family. It's equally true that nobody in his right mind would travel anywhere on Labor Day weekend. So what were my wife and I and our younger daughter doing in a strange church in the Adirondacks on a Labor Day Sunday morning? The prospect of the ordeal just a few hours away—south on Route 9 and east on Route 4 over the Green Mountains in slow-moving, impatient, bumper-to-bumper traffic was more than enough to distract me from the lovely service and the lovely setting.

I was asking God for affirmation of what I'd angrily offered to do the evening before, because it was a cinch I wasn't going to get any approval from my wife. I was also dividing my attention more or less evenly among the trip ahead, the Old Testament reading, and the events of the previous evening, at which I'd been introduced to my wife's extended family. Just at that moment a small black spider appeared on the right elbow of the man sitting in front of me. The man wore a bright green sweater and was quite large and solid, with half an inch of black, curly hair hanging over his shirt collar. This was probably the last day of his vacation, and he'd no doubt be getting a haircut before lunch on Tuesday.

The spider paused briefly, surveying her options. Then she started up the green polyester arm. My wife, daughter, and I watched, fascinated, the Old Testament all but forgotten.

It had been quite a weekend already. It featured an incomplete gathering of a clan that had fractured some years before. So there was considerable trashing of absent ex-spouses and other relatives who hadn't made it. It was also my introduction to one particular branch of the family, and there had occurred a further rupture. I didn't know whether to apologize or not. My conscience was telling me, "Good for you!" My wife was saying, "How could you!" And my daughter was giving me the thumbs up whenever the subject arose, as it frequently had.

The little black spider of St. Peter's-by-the-Lake reached the bend of the raglan shoulder in the middle of the Psalm and paused again to look about. This summer chapel was an ideal home for a spider. The congregation, which ran heavily to Izods and Topsiders, and some of whom had arrived for church in varnished launches, occupied the place only ten Sundays each summer. The rest of the year, the unfinished knotty pine walls and rustic vaults must have been ideal for hanging webs and snaring drowsy flies.

The Adirondacks is as near to a home as my wife

and I are likely to have. These mountains, where we first set up housekeeping, come as close as any place could. When we stop for coffee or fuel and listen, we know we're home. The old Irish diphthong *oi* is more pronounced here than anywhere in New England; as in "What toim's it? Foiv yet?" There's also a sneaking suggestion of a *d* in the sound *th*, a suggestion that comes to flower as we move south through the state toward the scene of its perfection, Brooklyn. Anyway, it's home, and I'd broken a long-standing rule prohibiting Labor Day weekend travel to spend a couple of days with my wife's family at a small cabin near Old Forge.

My wife's mother was there, and a widowed aunt and her son and his wife and kids; people I'd inherited when I got married, all mixed together with a couple of Frisbees and a few cases of beer and crammed into a tiny summer cabin for dinner. Except for my mother-in-law, they were relatives I'd never met before—and never would again, if I had anything to say about it.

My wife made a huge lasagna; the aunt ordered in four pizzas the size of lumber-wagon wheels; her son provided and exhibited a great personal interest in the cases of beer. There were kids hollering everywhere, and all the adults talked and shouted at each other at once. For some reason, the TV set was playing loudly; powerboats roared on one side of the camp, and traffic rumbled on the other. The apotheosis of the great American weekend! I faced it with the enthusiasm I normally reserve for the dentist's chair. But this was my wife's family, and for her sake I would not be grumpy all evening.

We called the kids in for supper. Our daughter, who at ten was almost too old to be playing with the little kids, sat next to me. "Having a good time?" I asked her.

"Yeah," she said. "We were playing a game with Uncle Ralph that was kind of funny. Like tag and hide-and-go-seek together. He called it 'catch the coon.' What's a coon?"

Uh-oh! "I'll tell you later," I said. I determined to keep an eye on Ralph, who was assuming the red-faced air of a belligerent drunk. My wife, I noticed, was watching him, too, and waggling her eyebrows at me in the way that means keep cool and keep your mouth shut!

We dined, with the kids climbing over us in the hot little room to get at the pizza and cold Cokes. After supper someone proposed a game of Trivial Pursuit. Oh, brother! This would be awful! But we chose up sides and went at it.

Surprisingly, the youngest team was cleaning everybody else's clock. They were really good at it. But they weren't being too diplomatic; they giggled and guffawed at their elders' occasional dumb answers. Ralph, who was almost through his second six-pack, was virtually glowing, but it was not with bonhomie. More like Vesuvius.

A few minutes later the question was, "What holiday do we celebrate on January 15?"

It was the kids' turn. "Martin Luther King Day!" they shouted triumphantly.

Ralph suddenly erupted in his lawn chair in the corner. "Pretty sad day," he rumbled darkly, "when we celebrate the birthday of a goddamn coon!"

There followed a sudden, shocked silence; then a flurry of older-woman talk as almost everybody tried to pretend he hadn't heard it. But not our daughter, God bless her! Raised in the academic atmosphere of Hanover, New Hampshire, she'd never heard that kind of language before. "Hey!" she shouted. "You can't talk like that!"

"By Jesus, I can! There's even some of 'em trying to stay in my motel almost every week. 'Fore you know it, they'll be taking over."

"But you can't talk like that. They're just like us . . . " She's not exactly a slip of a girl, but she looked like a bantam hen fluffed up at a—well, at a raccoon, now that I think of it.

Trying very hard to act just like Jimmy Stewart in a showdown, I said, "Ralph, maybe you and I ought to go out in the yard and talk about this."

Well, that line brought down the house! There were suddenly women everywhere, patting heads and shoulders, their hands fluttering, tut-tutting. Peace was restored, sort of. Ralph left a couple of minutes later—his wife wouldn't let their kids ride with him—and the evening descended into embarrassed reflection. My mother-in-law got in a last biting dig as we broke up and headed for bed. "It's a good thing for you he didn't go outside. You'd have gotten licked!" My own mother-in-law, for Pete's sake!

About halfway through the General Thanksgiving, the little black spider stepped from the shirt collar just in front of me to the ruddy skin above it. The three of us watching held our breath, but the big man appeared not to feel the footsteps. Up the spider climbed, over the point of the jawbone and past the earlobe. And finally a large, languid, hairy hand came up to brush away what it supposed to be a fly. The spider disappeared.

I sympathized. She should have stayed home Labor Day weekend, too.

The Defense of "Mother"

FOR YEARS NOW, IN SPEAKING TO VARIOUS audiences or writing in my newspaper column, I've referred to my wife as "Mother." As a result, I get occasional e-mails from (usually young) women, protesting that "Mother" is a demeaning epithet, that I'm from the Jurassic period, and doesn't she have a name? Likewise, every so often some woman in a supermarket checkout line or at a Rotary meeting will look twice at Mother, make the connection, and ask. "Are you 'Mother'?" And when that's affirmed, "Don't you mind being called 'Mother'? I mean, it's so . . . !"

Well, actually, she doesn't, and she says so when asked. And not just because that's been her name here at home since our oldest child began to talk, about forty years ago. Both of us have for years sort of turned the question aside. But it seems to have become a problem for some listeners and readers. So I've prepared a brief response that I've entitled, "The Defense of Mother."

For some reason, I've been an enthusiastic reader of editorial pages since I was quite young. As a kid, I regularly read Drew Pearson, Westbrook Pegler, Walter Winchell, Eric Sevareid, and Earl Wilson. Each of them had his specialty. Pegler, for example, wanted Eleanor Roosevelt wiped off the face of the earth; and Wilson, in his Broadway-beat column, often referred to his wife as "BW," which was short for "Beautiful Wife." I always found that far too cute for words, and I vowed to avoid that sort of thing if it ever came my turn.

Well, in recent years it has, so I've had to come up with a name for her. It's not possible that I wouldn't mention her. You've heard, no doubt, that astronomers can sometimes find previously undiscovered planets by measuring their gravitational effect upon planets they've already found. Well, that's the way it is with me and Mother: Our association so profoundly affects my orbit that not to mention her would be like leaving Venus out of the solar system; there'd be something vital missing.

But here is an intensely private person married to a rather public person, and the attention she gets by it isn't always welcome. Sometimes, if she's spotted and asked if she's my wife, she'll say, "Well, yes, I'm his first wife." Which usually quiets things right down.

So, because she's private, she doesn't want her real name used. It's inappropriate that I use in public the familiar sobriquet I use at home. I wouldn't use a pseudonym. And I refer to her as "my wife" only when the context of the sentence would make "Mother" confusing or ambiguous; I don't like the implication of proprietorship in "my wife." There are only two choices left.

She was seven years older than the next of her five sisters, in a family that was not—as I have mentioned elsewhere—consistently supportive and nurturing of its children. So from a very early age—for almost sixty years now—she's been a mother, first by default and later by choice. She can recall her own mother coming home from the hospital with the third of her sisters, a football-size premature infant they'd barely saved. "Here!" said her mother, holding the baby out. "You want this kid to live, you take care of her."

So never mind that now she's "Gramma" to four kids who call her about once a week. Never mind that, once her kids were on their own, she went into business for herself and has done quite well; or that she was once Rotarian of the Year. Around here she'll always be Mother.

I won't be disingenuous and pretend I don't know that the use of the term is an old New England tradition, and that therefore I don't find it even more appealing.

I easily forgive young people who find the title demeaning, but I could find the implication insulting. If there's a more important and critical position in this world than that of mother, I'd like to know what it is. Of all the things you could be, and be well—senator, president, pope, general, pastor, doctor, professor, artist—none is as demanding or as important in the grand scheme of things as mother.

So to me it's not just a name I automatically call her; it's also a gesture of profound respect and gratitude.

But I said back there that there were two choices. She suggested them years ago when we were discussing this subject. The other was "Her Majesty." That's even worse than BW! So I'm sticking with Mother.

I just hope she'll stick with me.

Mother's Day in Court

"UH-OH, WHAT'S THIS?" I ASKED. There was a little official-looking piece of paper on Mother's desk. When I reached for it, she snatched it away.

"I am not guilty!" she cried.

"Guilty of what? What is this?"

"You know perfectly well what it is, or you wouldn't have noticed. It's a traffic ticket. They say I went through a Stop sign. But I'm not guilty, and I'm not going to pay the fine!"

"What Stop sign?"

"The one at the end of Partridge Road, where it meets Trescott."

"Well, did you run the sign or not?"

"It's out of sight. You can't see it until you get right on top of it because it's around the corner." I couldn't help but notice that she hadn't answered the question. But why mention it?

We recently completed a Lenten study course, she and I, down at church. It was based on a system of personality analysis called the Myers-Briggs Type Indicator Test. Some of you have probably had experience with it. A brief, written, multiple-choice test indicates whether you are: extroverted or introverted; rely on your senses or your intuition; lead with your head or with your heart; prefer things planned and settled or open and flexible.

Among the items churned out by the computer after it digests your test results are a personal profile and several paragraphs called "some simple exercises . . . (to) make you more effective in your personal dealings." Naturally, it's more fun to read the former than the latter.

It was interesting for me to see, for example, that, true to the old adage, opposites do indeed attract. The system calls them "complements," which is probably a better way to put it. Apparently, each of us instinctively fills out his hand with the cards he hasn't got by marrying them. Mother and I obviously managed to do that; we're virtually polar opposites in the ways we perceive and go at things.

And here was a perfect opportunity to check it out: a traffic ticket.

Now, if I'd gotten it, it would have been an entirely different situation. As "an extrovert concerned for people's feelings," I try to establish personal relationships with the local cops—who are generally pretty nice guys—and thus obey the traffic laws (when I do) more out of concern for that relationship than for fear of tickets or causing an accident. If I'd gotten that ticket (which I wouldn't have—I know the sign's there, and I always stop for Stop signs), I'd either have paid it or, if I felt genuinely that the sign was obscured, I'd have called the chief to complain gently. If he'd been unresponsive, I'd have paid the fine.

But I didn't get the ticket. Here's who did: "a self-confident and individualistic thinker [who draws her] view of the way things are from within, from the 'inner eye' to reality: intuition." And Mother's intuition told her she wasn't guilty. So I braced myself. I could see this going all the way to the Supreme Court.

For over forty years now, in situations like this, I've played the devil's advocate: Have you thought of this, and that, and what about the . . . ? And in this situation it seemed more than ever appropriate. I should ask her the kinds of damning questions the judge was likely to ask.

But I didn't. And it was because of what I'd learned from the course we'd just finished. It was impossible for me to think of a courtroom situation without wondering what the other people there were feeling and likely to ask or say; it was just as impossible for her to care. "You turn all your energy toward achieving your goal, regardless of any obstacles," reads her profile. "In fact, you ignore the obstacles." So I just asked how I could help.

Watching her prepare her defense was like watching Clarence Darrow or F. Lee Bailey with a celebrated client. Telephone calls to state agencies, the state police, and state highway departments. (Nobody in the State of New Hampshire, apparently, knows the distance from which a Stop sign has to be visible, though all agree there must be a law about it somewhere.) We made visits to the scene of the alleged infraction. We reenacted the incident at a legal speed and attempted to stop after the sign became visible.

Finally, we spent a good half hour at the scene with a camera and color film, recording every view. When the pictures came back, she tacked them in sequence on a corkboard.

"You know how long this is taking you to get ready?" I asked. "And how much it's costing for all the visual aids? Be cheaper to pay the fine."

Those are not necessarily stupid comments; they're the things my type would've been thinking about. For all the effect they had on Mother, they might as well have been stupid. This was not a matter of strategy or pragmatism, but one purely of principle.

Court day arrived, and she was ready for battle—on her terms. Then, at the last moment before leaving—though clad in the armor of righteousness and armed with photographic evidence of the "facts"—she briefly broke character. Like a child afraid to venture alone into a dark bedroom, she asked her extrovert, sensing, feeling husband to go with her for support. On the way down, we stopped at the scene one last time and paced off the distances shown in her photographs.

We sat in the anteroom at the courthouse. And sat some more. I read a newspaper; she vibrated. A DUI case preceded hers. The defendant had a lawyer, so it took a lot of time. When it was finally over, one of the local police officers motioned her to a corner of the hall. "The ticketing officer in your case is out of the state on an investigation," he informed her, "and since it's such a minor matter, we're not going to continue it. It's discharged."

"It's what?" she cried. "But I have all these pictures!" Holy Toledo! I couldn't believe this! Been me, I'd have been out of there like a shot. But not her. She set up her corkboard right there in the hall, and for the next few minutes the assembled officers were subjected to what would have been her defense had the case been pressed. They agreed that, yep, she had a point there. As the sensitive person in our partnership, though, I could perceive that their body language disagreed.

"You see," she said on the way home, "I was right."

"Of course you were. I never doubted it." I smiled to myself, recalling the biblical formula regarding two individuals becoming one. Actually, I thought, they may become one, but they also become much more than two. Together, we are a nation.

The Baby Leaves

MANY YEARS AGO, WHEN OUR YOUNGER daughter, the baby of the family, was four years old, Mother took her to nursery school. That first day, they walked in together to meet the teachers and the other kids. But the next day, when they pulled up out front, the baby said, "This is my school, and I can go in by myself." She jogged up the walk, tugged the heavy door open just wide enough to squeeze through, and disappeared inside. She never once looked back.

Our house seems like a mausoleum tonight. It's not that it's all that quiet. I can hear most of the usual noises: the television set downstairs, the creak of my swivel chair when I lean back, the soft hum of the electric clock. But there's something important missing. I've become accustomed to a muted throbbing not quite beneath the consciousness of this house— the *boom-boom* of rock music, like the mutter of distant jungle drums. Tonight it is silent, as it was all day. And as it will be tomorrow morning.

In addition, there's a sort of brownout in the energy level of the place. A set of footsteps is missing. The pen here on my desk is right where I left it this morning; the phone hasn't rung all evening; and there are no shoes, lacrosse sticks, or overdue library books scattered around the front hall.

The baby has left. After twenty-seven years, Mother and I are alone in the house. Which is not too unusual. But for the first time ever we're not waiting for someone to come home.

This didn't sneak up on us at all. We were as ready for it as ever we could have been, and it feels just the way we thought it would. It's just that anticipating how it will feel and actually feeling it are two quite different things.

A friend of mine once said that he saw our lives as divided roughly into three parts. For the first third we're kids, growing up and learning; during the second, we're working and raising kids of our own; and for the last third we're sort of tapering off and enjoying the fruits of our labors and our child-rearing. So this is enjoyment, hey? When does it quit feeling like a missing molar?

Poor Jerry the Cat seems equally affected by it. Every once in a while he gets up, runs up the stairs, and walks several times around the baseboards of the baby's room with his head hanging down. He sniffs at the unusually neat bedclothes, takes a turn through the little bathroom, and yowls a few times. He knows what's happened. Then he thumps slowly back downstairs, where he walks in more circles until one of us scoops him up. He suffers us to try to console him because we're all right. But we're not missing.

For about the last year, since the baby got her driver's license, Mother and I have had a little game: It's 11 o'clock; do you know where your car is? Now, suddenly the game is over. The car is in the yard. And the gas tank, which I was sure had a bad leak, turns out to be intact, after all.

The ice cream game is over, too. It's always been considered boorish bad form in our family to finish off the ice cream in the freezer. So it had become a game to *almost* finish the ice cream. One of us would leave, say, a tablespoonful in a half-gallon carton; the next would leave a teaspoonful; and so on down to the smallest indivisible particle still recognizable as ice cream. Thus, when Mother reached into the freezer for some dessert, took a look, and roared, "Who finished off the ice cream?" nobody answered. For nobody had literally finished it off. I'm afraid the game is over for good. I'm going to miss that one, too.

In June she graduated from high school, but she pleaded for a fifth year—a sort of transition year—in a small prep school about fifty miles away. Just far enough to be away, but close enough to be not too far to drive if the need arose. And last Saturday was finally The Day.

So on a gray morning we drove down the Connecticut Valley on the first leg of a journey that will lead who knows where. The routine, once we got there, was comfortable and comforting: registration, books, reception, lugging baggage up to the room, lunch, orientation for new parents, and then—suddenly—orientation for new students and time for Mother and me to go. We were the spent rocket boosters on our little shuttle, and the second stage was about to fire.

We hugged quickly, awkwardly in a parking lot. It was starting to drizzle. Then the baby—transformed magically into a young lady almost late for an important meeting—turned and walked away and into a nearby building. And just as she hadn't many years ago, she didn't look back.

Mother and I drove home through thickening rain and spent the afternoon moping around the empty house. Just before supper I started a fire in the downstairs stove to take the chill off, and we ate quietly, the cat rubbing against our ankles.

At 10:30 that night, as I reconciled my August bank statement, the phone on my desk rang.

"Dad? Can you believe it? I forgot my lacrosse stick! And the typewriter! Is there any way you can get them down to me?"

The next morning at 7:30, as I sipped a cup of coffee and read the newspaper, the phone rang again: "Dad? I'm sorry to keep bothering you, but I'm going out for soccer. I need my cleats in my closet. And some more coat hangers. Is Mom there? Before she comes to the phone, have her get a pencil and a piece of paper, will you? Thanks!"

Mother and I decided to wait a week or two before we began the last third of our lives.

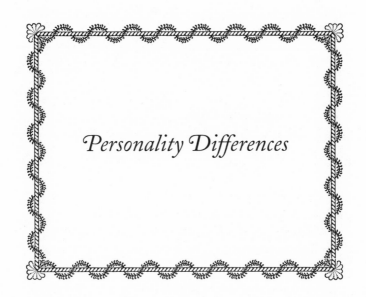

Personality Differences

Marriage and a Ferryboat

WHEN I WAS A LITTLE KID, MY FATHER told me that when a boat crosses a line visible only on a chart, like a meridian or a state border, the passengers often can feel a slight bump. I knew even then when he told me that it was just foolishness; but still, I sort of stand easy and quiet on the observation deck as the ferryboat *Governor Aiken* passes the midpoint of Lake Champlain. You never know . . .

Ahead of us loom the Green Mountains, with the summits of Mansfield and Camel's Hump in the clouds. Behind us, emerging from the foothills as we near the Vermont shore, rise the Adirondacks, flagged with tattered snow showers and shafts of slanting sunlight. A northwest wind drives down the lake, and the ferry lifts its port quarter to the rollers. Four arctic terns—probably parents with two kids— flit by in close formation, their wing tips seeming to touch the water. In a few weeks they'll leave in time to greet spring in Tierra del Fuego.

This crossing of the lake, from Essex, New York, to Charlotte, Vermont, never fails to rouse old memories, both historical and personal. The first European exploration of the North American interior began here in the summer of 1609, when Samuel de Champlain emerged from the head of the Richelieu

River. He named the lake for himself, killed several Iroquois Indian chiefs with his harquebus—an epic strategic blunder—and noted the presence of a large sea serpent.

Then followed over one hundred years of war, as the British and French, and later the Americans, chased each other up and down the lake. The route of our throbbing little ferryboat crosses the wakes of Rogers' Rangers, Benedict Arnold, Gentleman Johnny Burgoyne, Thomas MacDonough, and, more recently, the bootlegger Mushrat Robare. Kids still dig British cannonballs out of the bluffs at the mouth of the Boquet River, and an occasional bottle of Canadian whiskey from the sandbars just off-shore.

This is also the country where my wife and I began our family and our own humble history some years ago. We built our first house here in 1964, in a patch of white pines atop a limestone outcrop. We still stay there with old friends whenever we come back to visit—often for weddings or funerals. Looking back at it now, I'm amazed at our youthful innocence and energy.

This time the visit was for a wedding: the baby, now grown up, of a large family whose oldest kids were once students of mine. The bride and groom looked so young!—like kids in a high school play—yet they were years older than we'd been when we were married.

It's also the weekend of our anniversary, which made the occasion, with its fervent vows of undying fidelity until death, all the more poignant for us. As most older folks know, only people with more hope than experience can look each other in the eye and unabashedly repeat those vows with no other thoughts going through their minds. Watching them, I hoped that life would be kind.

Wedding anniversaries are for celebrating, I suppose—for sending cards and flowers, and going out to eat someplace special, and getting phone calls from your family. But they're also, as now on the observation deck of the *Governor Aiken,* with millennia of history and the hills of home in view, a time for reflecting, summing up, evaluating.

While I'm up here peering to windward like (I fancy) Sir Francis Drake, Mother is down in the car snoozing. It's not that she's sleepy. She has a very active imagination; and if she gets up here, she begins to picture the boat rolling over, exploding, or striking a submerged object and sinking in less than a minute, leaving us to struggle in the icy, wave-tossed waters till, tragically, we drown. I picture the same catastrophe, but my scenario runs more to the heroic. Just to make sure, I step over to the life raft canister and read the inflation and launching instructions.

What makes a marriage? I don't know. But I do know that when the last of the kids leaves, and all the energy and resources you spent on them are now available for other purposes, you really discover what you've been becoming all those years. And I must say, it's been quite a bit of fun.

I love flying, and the smaller the plane, the better; Mother, when I can get her anywhere near a plane, can lift a 757 off the ground all by herself by pulling up on the armrests. She loves shopping; I detest it. I keep inching the heat lever on the car dashboard downward; she always slides it all the way up and turns on the fan, besides. And the list goes on. In fact, I can't easily think of anything we both like, except maybe the first sip out of a bottle of cold beer, and there's only one of those. Yet when I see another couple togged out for a mutual interest—binoculared for birding, or wet-suited for diving, black-tied and gowned for a concert, or Lycra clad for cycling—I feel pity mixed with my envy.

I always feel that they're missing something: an opposing point of view. When someone shares your interests, you argue the fine points; when he does not, you argue philosophy and gain perspective. Thus over the years, Mother and I have gained a great deal of perspective.

For example, when I hear a certain cry from the woods—*"Cack-cack-cack-cack"*—I whisper excitedly, "Hear that? *Dryocopus pileatus!*"

"That's nice." She yawns. "Did you pay that furnace-cleaning bill yet?"

Opposites attract and complement each other. If they didn't, we wouldn't have magnets or electric motors or lightning, and Mother and I wouldn't be married. Each serves, alternately, as the pendulum to the other's mainspring. It was not for nothing that Providence prevented me from marrying someone like myself. This marriage has at times been difficult; that one would have been impossible.

We're coming into the Vermont slip. Time to go back down, start the car, and head for home. Should

I jump on the bumper as I go by and scare her? I've got about ten seconds to decide.

I could tell her it's just the boat crossing the Vermont state line. But I'll bet she knows that's out in the middle of the lake.

Painting the Bedroom

THE IDEA CRAWLED MONSTERLIKE FROM the black lagoon of my wife's fecund imagination.

It was Friday night bedtime. We'd made it through another week. A few more hours' work on Saturday would bring it to a successful close. We'd just gone to bed and had begun to doze. A big, round moon was rising over Moose Mountain, glittering on the snow-covered fields. The cross-country skiing Saturday afternoon would be perfect—the earliest in years. And just then the monster began to roil the surface of the lagoon.

I should have known she'd do something like this. She's always been this way: the living epitome of the maxim that humankind abhors an equilibrium. Pandora is her patron saint, and her watchword is "Never let sleeping dogs lie." That, in this case, meant me.

"I want to get this bedroom painted tomorrow," she said, as casually as if she meant to change the kitty litter.

The notion was clearly ridiculous. What kind of half-wit would do a thing like that right in the middle of getting ready for the holidays? So I drifted off to sleep chuckling indulgently. Next morning I was up and gone before she was even awake.

But when I came home at noon, there was a little

blue paint chip on the kitchen floor where I'd be sure to see it. Next to it, a note: *Pls get 2 gals flt latex, 2 qts low enamel this color xactly. If cant match, go lightr. If you love me and rely want to show it, start ptng ASAP. Home soon. Love.*

You ever tried arguing with a note? Especially one that says, "If you love me . . . " What a dirty trick! So I didn't argue. Off I went to the hardware store.

I couldn't match the color exactly, of course. So the paint man and I, as directed, picked a color a little lighter, mixed up the right amount, and I took it home.

Now you have to understand that there's a vast and basic difference between what my wife means by painting a room and what I mean. To her, it's simply a matter of pulling the furniture a foot or so away from the walls, throwing down a newspaper or an old towel, and starting to paint—using one of those awful little triangular plastic-mounted sponges that you dip into a roller pan and then slide around on the wall. "Saturday Morning Specials," I call them—the cheap handguns of the amateur painting crowd.

She also paints like a television paint commercial: lunch in the green room, dinner in the red room. I knew she planned to sleep in the blue room that night.

But to me, painting a room means first removing all the furniture, then covering the whole floor with drop cloths, and masking the carpet at the baseboards with tape and newspapers. Next, remove all the hardware and electrical cover plates with a screwdriver, stowing all the pieces in a two-pound coffee can. And then you begin. But not painting. First you have to go over the walls with spackle or joint compound, filling nail holes, recovering popped drywall nails, puttying cracks in the trim joints. Then you let it all dry, before sanding and washing the whole thing down with warm, soapy water. Let it dry again. And finally you're ready to begin with the paint.

Thus, when she came home from work about two, the dressers were choking the hallway, the bed was in the family room between the stove and the humidifier, her desk was in the bathroom, and the contents of the closets were all over the living room. Up to my elbows in soapy water, I was in a decidedly ugly mood. "What are you doing?" she shrieked, and like an old football coach, I could see it was going to be a long afternoon.

I suppose I could have been conciliatory or apologetic, but I was feeling like neither. "What do you mean, what am I doing?" I fired back. "You want me to paint right over these cobwebs?" This last delivered with heavy irony.

It went right over her head. "Of course!" she answered. "Isn't that why you paint a bedroom?" Breathing noisily through her nose, she left to dig out her painting clothes from under the piles in the living room.

Soon a cry from the kitchen: "What's this?" She'd found the paint. "Why didn't you match the chip I gave you?"

"Couldn't. But you said to get a lighter shade if we couldn't, so I did."

"I don't know. It looks awfully blue to me."

At eleven that night the joint compound still wasn't dry enough to sand. So we made up the bed in the family room and slept out there—on extreme opposite sides of the mattress.

After early church on Sunday, I started to sand my patch job. My wife opened a can of paint and began to flourish her sponge pad.

"Hold it!" I cried. "After I finish this, we have to go around with the vacuum and a damp cloth. Otherwise you'll have dust in your paint job." She muttered something rude as she left for the vacuum cleaner, but within half an hour we were finally ready to begin.

Sunlight streamed in the windows. She smeared away on one side of the room with her sponge, and I splattered away with my roller on the other. I could see that I'd be done in plenty of time for a good, long ski that afternoon, and we'd have the furniture back by bedtime. I hummed happily at my work.

"Stop!" she said suddenly. I stopped and turned around.

"Just look at that blue!" she wailed. "How could you do it? It looks like a circus wagon!"

Well, I had to admit it was a little bright (but only where it was dry). So we stopped. And yesterday morning she went to the hardware store herself to get the color just the way she wanted it. Maybe by next weekend, if we're lucky, we'll be done.

Meanwhile, we're still sleeping in the family room and using the living room as a closet. I sure hope we get sorted out soon. Though I'm rather getting to like painting a little during the evenings and then going to bed between the humidifier and the stove. It's kind of like living in a rain forest on the side of a volcano. Paul Gauguin, if he were still with us, would love it.

Dancing with the Telemarketers

IN WELL OVER FORTY YEARS OF MARRIAGE, Mother and I have voted the same way only once; in every other election, we've nullified each other's vote. We feel passionate about certain politicians and about our political positions, so much so that we've had to come to a truce: If she will not allude in a derogatory way to the character of our recent past president, I will make no comments about the performance of the present one.

Because we don't discuss politics, I often think, as Election Day approaches, that she may have forgotten it. But when I get to the polls, there's the telltale check beside her name. Damn!

She uses a PC, and I've got a Mac (that she calls "a toy computer"). I use a terrific local server, so of course she uses AOL. I'm a pretty liberal, pointy-headed, intellectual Democrat; she's definitely not. So we approach virtually every problem and situation from opposite points of view and with different technologies.

One problem we had for many years was telemarketers. Whenever one of those awful people called us at dinnertime trying to sell us something, we responded according to type. "Young man" (or woman, whichever the case), I would say, "couldn't you have found some gainful employment that would be of some benefit to society, rather than this irritating and quite inconvenient thing that you're doing? If you'd like, I can suggest a job counselor in your area who . . . " and so on. She, on the other hand, if interrupted in either dinner preparation or dining, simply shouted, "Why don't you get a respectable job or go back on welfare!" and slammed down the phone.

Neither approach worked. Mine simply prolonged the fruitless pleading, and hers elicited a follow-up call asking her to listen, at least, to the offer.

No more. We may agree on few things, but one of them is what to do when one of these bozos calls. They have databases and know a lot about you before they call—your name and phone number (obviously), your town, age, Social Security number, and the average income in your Zip code area. In an effort to be folksy, they guess at your nickname. They always guess wrong on mine. Somehow, they also know when Mother's been to the butcher and bought spare ribs, because they always call the next night, when my fingers are covered in barbecue sauce. So when I answer the phone, I'm already angry.

"Hello!" I shout into the phone.

Some guy from a former Confederate state shouts back, but in a slightly different tone, "Hah, Beeyul! How's the weatha up yonder?"

Up yonder, my ass! I've got one of those unspeakable creatures on the line! This is the point at which I used to go into my bleeding-heart job-counseling routine. But, as I said, we've found our old responses next to useless. Besides which, these characters almost always call at supper time during the winter. They know that anybody in New England, if he has any sense at all, is indoors after dark in the winter.

What they don't know is that there's nothing going on after dark in Etna in any season, either indoors or out. We live on a dead-end dirt road; nobody comes up here but people who live here. Nobody drops by. How are you going to drop by on a dead-end road? We get fewer than two channels of TV, and the reception is awful. In January, you can look at the TV screen or out the window; it's the same show on both of 'em. Used to be we had a high old time about once a month: standing the kids up against the kitchen doorjamb and making a mark—Ginny, 7/2/75—but the kids are long gone now, so we can't do that. The dog doesn't say boo, and a fisher killed our cat. There's not really much going on up our road.

So we've agreed to treat these callers differently. Now, whoever gets the call raises his eyebrows and index finger, and the other one starts his wrist stopwatch. Because now the trick is not to get rid of them, but to see which of us can keep them on the line the longest without buying anything. We've never bought a thing from them, and we're never going to—much less give out a credit card number over the phone—but what else is there that's going on up our road? There's nothing much worse than cold, gray, greasy barbecue. But now we've got a microwave, I can just pop it back in there when I'm finally off the phone.

So this guy says, "Hah, Beeyul. How's the weatha up yonder?" and I raise my index finger to start the timer. Now, I know he's looking at his database, and he's asking himself, "What in the world can Etna, New Hampshire, possibly be? Just a godforsaken little one-horse village full of dumb farmers and loggers? And this guy, he's sixty-seven years old, probably just came in from the barn and still smells like it; dumber'n a post; half his teeth; and a credit card. I can sell this guy!" No, he can't. But he doesn't know it yet.

I know what he thinks he's got, so that's what he gets: deaf, stupid, and grumpy. And he discovers right away that I take forever to process information.

So, after he asks about the weather and I've given Mother the high sign to start timing, I pause for several long seconds. Then I say, in the voice of an old man, "Who . . . ah, who's this?"

"This's Ralph Underhill, Beeyul!"

Long pause. Then, "Who . . . ah, who'd you say 'twas?" I can ask this question three or four times, and eat up a full minute, before poor Ralph is shouting his name so loud that Mother can hear it, clear across the kitchen.

"Yas, yas, Underhill. You ain't got to shout. I can hear ya. Now, where, ah . . . where you callin' from, Mr. . . . .ah, what'd you say your name . . . oh, never mind. Where you callin' from?"

"Atlanta, Beeyul!"

Long silence while I digest that startling bit of information. Then: "Atlanta-beeyul, eh? Well now, ya know, I've heard of Mobile, but I ain't never heard . . . "

"No, no, no! Atlanta, Georgia!"

"Oh . . . whyn't you say so? Well, just a minute, will you, Mr. . . . .what'd you say your name . . . oh, never mind." Then, shouting over my shoulder, "Sweetheart! Would you see if you can't find that road atlas? I think maybe it's up in the back bedroom." Back into the phone: "I'm gonna have Mother go see if she can't find the road atlas, because neither one of us has any idea where Atlanta . . . "

This guy is in for it just as long as he can stand it. Finally he tells himself whatever he sells this old half-wit can't be worth the aggravation. *Bang!* he slams the phone down, and I raise my index finger again. Right on the wall beside where the kids' heights go up, there's a list coming down: date, who took the call, who called, what he was selling, and how long we kept him on the line. After a few years, we've developed quite an impressive list there.

I'm pretty good at this, if I do say so myself. But Mother! She's the Obi-wan Kenobi of the telephone. Watching her work is like watching Sarah Bernhardt play Lady Macbeth. Mother used to be a telephone operator back in the fifties, when operators—you've seen the pictures—when they had headphones and a lapful of snakes they kept plugging in and pulling out. Nothing rattles her on the telephone. She's deadly to these guys.

Just like me, she's deaf, stupid, and grumpy. But she adds interested, which just kills these folks; they know they're going to sell her something. Just like me, she's originally from New York State, but when she's on the phone with a salesperson, she goes into such a song and dance, she sounds like a Pepperidge Farm commercial. And she uses language that hasn't been heard in the United States since maybe the second Cleveland administration—like "By scissors!" or "I do vum!" If I dare to raise my eyebrows at such incredible anachronisms, she claps the phone to her chest and hisses, "M.Y.O.B.!"

Just like me, she stalls for time to run the clock, but she doesn't use long silences the way I do. "Any idiot," she says pointedly, "can just stand there and say nothing, as if he were thinking." She's right, of course, but fails to appreciate that it takes a superb sense of timing to know how long even an idiot can sustain that silence. What she does is, she pretends she's got a stammer; she's discovered that nobody, not even a telemarketer, ever hangs up on a stammer-er. It can take her a full two minutes to ask the caller if it's true she can actually chop carrots, knead bread, and mash potatoes in the appliance he's pitching. When he assures her she can, she exclaims, "Wal, I swan!"—this with a dangerous look at me to keep my trap shut.

Finally you can tell the guy's boss is pointing to a time clock on the other end and whispering, "Geez, you gotta get off the line! You been on over fifteen minutes!" Because I can sense her kind of backing away from the phone,

"Yas, yas," she says, "I think so. Eyah. One fer, fer, fer me and the old fa-, old fa-, old man and one fer, fer each of the kids. Eyup. There's six a them." And you can just picture the guy on the other end, exulting: Yes! I sold seven of these damn things!

"Yep, I'll have Fa-, Fa-, Father go get the cre-, cred-it card. But while he's gone, let me ast ya a question. That thing you're sellin'—don't it take 'lectricity?"

Soon as she says that, I can hit the stopwatch. He's gone, and he's never coming back. And once again she's skunked me, in duration of call and on style points, besides. It's a losing battle.

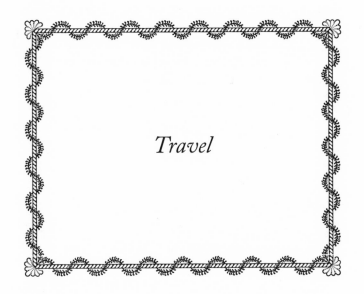

Travel

The Vacation from Hell

It would be difficult to say what exactly was the high point of that vacation; there were several. But certainly the most memorable was the point at which, up to my waist in ice water several miles off the coast of Maine, surrounded by floating red gas cans, I realized the boat wasn't going to right herself unless I could somehow release the sheets. And it was at that moment I heard my wife's anxious cry from below: "Will! There's water coming out of the fireplace!"

Mother, in her most charitable moods, refers to that week as not one of my most inspired ideas. In a similar mood, I am likely to imply that her usual spirit of sportsmanship seemed to fail her just when it was most needed. But we do agree completely on a title for this thrilling little chapter in our lives: The Vacation from Hell.

When I think about it, it still seems like a great idea. The kids were old enough to be left with a sitter for several days; we were heading into the summer a few bucks ahead for a change; and I'd done quite a bit of open boat sailing off the coast of Maine in my days as an Outward Bound instructor. So, when I saw an ad describing a 26-foot cutter for charter in Brooklin, Maine, I proposed a romantic little getaway at sea.

It was quite a few years ago, but I still recall that she asked very few questions and agreed fairly readily to go. I should have been suspicious that she wasn't suspicious enough of an idea with the potential for the ultimate catastrophe. But I was so tickled that she'd said yes, I never once wondered if there wasn't a hidden agenda somewhere among the stuff she packed for the trip. There was.

A 26-footer isn't too much of a sailboat, and this one had a slight list to port and very little headroom. But to me she was the *Bluenose,* the *Spray,* and *Gypsy Moth* all rolled into one. We ferried our gear out to her in the little dinghy provided, raised the sails, dropped the mooring, and headed eagerly westward up Eggemoggin Reach.

A cutter isn't a sloop, which is what I was used to. It has two headsails instead of one, which means you can drive it hard without fighting the helm. But it also means that in a puff, you can't just let go the tiller and have it head safely up into the wind all by itself. This I had yet to learn. First came the surfing lesson.

We approached the head of the Reach, where it opened to the south, to the full length of Penobscot Bay. Till now we'd enjoyed the shelter of Little Deer Isle to windward, but looking ahead to Pumpkin Island Light, I could see a southerly gale whipping the whitecaps into spindrift. Wisely, I doused the staysail; foolishly, I stuck my nose out into the bay.

Holy Toledo! Probably the only thing that saved our lives that afternoon was the fact that Bucks Harbor was dead downwind of us. We found out later we'd come through fifty knots of wind. I found out right then that when a sailboat is surfing downwind, virtually out of control, a fifty-yard-wide harbor mouth looks more like a five-foot-wide needle's eye.

It's not quite true the boat was out of control; it's just that there were no options at all to what we were doing. Mother went below, where she alternately prayed and called up on deck to ask how we were doing. I told her each time, of course, that we were doing just fine, which didn't seem to reassure her. Perhaps it was my falsetto voice.

Ten minutes later, safe in the lee of the harbor island, we picked up a mooring on the first try, and the gale was but a memory. We rowed ashore and did Bucks Harbor. There was nothing to see or do that we could afford, so we went back aboard and cooked supper.

As we sat drinking our coffee after supper, I noticed that Mother hadn't lit up a smoke as usual. Instead, she held an infant pacifier in her hand, which she popped into her mouth after each sip of coffee. And beside her on the bunk lay a bottle of Nicoban. So that was it! After twenty-two years of a steady habit, she'd picked this voyage as the occasion to go cold turkey. It was easy to see why she would, but damn! It was the best of times to do it, perhaps. But it was also the worst of times.

The next day was worse. Sailing south in a freshening offshore breeze, I was still getting used to the boat, and we got flattened. It scared the daylights out of both of us. Mother, suffering from the pangs of withdrawal and the certainty of imminent death, got seasick over the side and went below again. At which point we really got knocked down, and the sea water, flowing down the chimney on the port side, began gushing from the fireplace in the cabin.

The sheets were jam-cleated to leeward, of course, which was now underwater. But a quick, messy dive freed them, and we righted once again. "Start the motor!" I called down the companionway.

"Start it!" she cried. "I don't even know where it is!"

She was right; I'd neglected to point it out the day before. So we shall draw a blind over the rest of that day and fast-forward to the evening. Tied fast to the town float in Rockland, and still alive, we lolled on the fantail, dropped spent lobster shells overside into the harbor, and tried to forget that we had four days' voyaging still to go.

Truly a remarkable vacation. And a watershed, too. Mother's never had a smoke since then; I've never tipped over a sailboat since then; and we've given up altogether on romantic voyages for two— except, perhaps, in a canoe. In calm, flat water. After mosquito season.

Short Separations Promote Long Unions

As I write these words this evening, I can't shake from my mind the thought that at this same moment, my wife is in great distress.

That's hard to believe, given the idyllic setting of our home during the month of May. The trees are budding; the skunk cabbage and the trout lilies are leafing out; and the forget-me-nots are in full bloom. My maniac lawn is rioting like eighteenth-century Parisians. There's a cock partridge down in the swamp who's been drumming even at night this past week; a pair of pileated woodpeckers is nesting somewhere on the property; and this morning I had to stop the truck to let a little timberdoodle hen and her six peewees cross the road at the foot of the driveway. Even the black flies aren't too bad yet. Things couldn't be much better. Yet I know that Mother's suffering, wherever she is.

She's left home. There's nobody here now but me and the cat. He's over on the daybed, gathering his strength for his nightly stampede around the house, and feeling kind of blue in his own way. He knows by now that open suitcases in bedrooms always portend loneliness; and there've been suitcases lying around here for over a week now. He senses that today he lost half his family, and that Mother's not coming back, at least for a while. If he knew what she was doing right now, he'd feel even worse.

Because at this moment she's about six miles above the North Atlantic, holding an Air France jet in the air solely by the pressure of her grip upon the arm rests of her seat. Outside the emergency exit she insisted upon sitting next to, the sky is black, though there should be a moon. If it's cloudy on the sea where she is, the moon is gleaming milk-white in the cumulus beneath the plane; if it's clear, it glints off the water even farther below. Either way, she's wondering about the temperature of the water—as if it made a difference.

When we were younger, Mother and I used to sniff with mild disdain at elderly people who took separate vacations. "Call that a marriage?" we asked each other rhetorically. "That'll never happen to us!"

Now that we're older, however, we can begin to see the wisdom of such things. We reserve our mild disdain nowadays for younger people who despair that they "don't enjoy the same things" and decide upon separation or divorce. How often we've heard, as if it were a justification, that so-and-so doesn't pursue the same interests that his or her spouse does. Or that "I don't like the person I become when I'm with him or her, doing his or her thing." Or that "I'm not reaching my full potential because of my involvement in this relationship." That, if it's sincere, betrays very little imagination.

Neither Mother nor I likes the person she becomes when we're doing my thing, mainly because

my thing usually involves snow, cold water, or mosquitoes. And we both despise the curmudgeon I
become when we do hers, which is almost always
associated with crowds, traffic lights, elevator music,
and tractor trailers passing on the right. As tense as
Mother may be tonight, it's nothing to what riding
with her to Boston does to me. A little beyond
Manchester, if the traffic's at all hectic, I invariably
curl up with a pillow and a magazine on the floor
behind the front seat and stay there until she finds a
parking place.

You can get all worked up about things like that
(and I'll admit that occasionally we do), or you can
mutually agree that, while it may be too bad it's true,
it isn't worth upsetting the apple cart over it. As Aunt
Therese (my Italian aunt, whom Mother once
referred to as the only human being in my whole
family) once said to us while we were fuming at each
other at a family gathering, "You two get too excited
about things that don't really make a difference." It's
far better for us to be apart for a little while than forever. So she's on her way to France with her two
daughters, and I'm right here where I want to be,
within half a mile of a good trout pond and in the
company of a pretty good cat. The mere idea of tooling through Provence with the three of them in a
French car the size of a roller skate gives me hives.

It's not that we never take trips and vacations
together; we usually do. But when there's so much at
stake, as in this one, and other options available, it
doesn't make a lot of sense. And this evening, when
she called me from Montreal to let me know that, in
spite of all odds and indications and her leaving

home an hour late, she'd made her plane, we reached a further tacit agreement: I think we agreed that, even when we go together, we'll leave at different times.

For weeks before a trip, I make a list of things to take—three ounces of baking soda, for example; or 108 inches of dental floss; two ballpoint pens; three ties (one pattern, one rep, one solid); the way normal people do. Then in the last hour before departure I take a shower, smugly stuff all that stuff on the list into a carry-on bag and a clothes bag, and plop it down by the front door with ten minutes to spare. What a guy!

Not her. Her last week at home reminds me of a border collie trying to get a huge flock through a little gate. "Lists!" she says. "Are you kidding?" She ignores Ernest Hemingway's advice about quitting work before you're done so you'll know where to start when you get back to it. She tries to do it all before she leaves. Meanwhile, piles of stuff begin to grow like mushrooms in various rooms. From time to time she herds them toward the front door.

I choose a departure time that allows for getting fuel, changing a flat tire on the road (which we've never yet experienced), and finding, on the way out of town, a 24-hour teller that works. She has a "target time," which, in spite of experience, I still take seriously. If we'd been leaving together today, I'd have been standing at the front door for an hour, tapping my foot and looking significantly at my watch, while she was still addressing letters, paying bills, and looking for the Tylenol. She'd have been irritated at the pressure, distracted, and then angry. I'd have been irritated, then anxious, then sarcastic, and then in deep trouble.

So she's off, and it's pretty lonesome around here. But better to be lonesome for a few days than for many years. And in just a couple of days I'll start making a list myself. I'm looking forward to a romantic tryst, as if with a lovely, dark-haired stranger, next Monday in the ruins of Pompeii.

Nude Descending a Ceiling

"THIS PLACE ALLOWS DOGS," ANNOUNCED Mother, emerging from the motel room in Sorel, Quebec. "So we're staying here for the night. But I want you to see this!" I got out of the van, grabbed the bags, and followed her into a tiny sitting room with a washroom and bedroom beyond. A strange reddish light emanated from the bedroom.

I went in. Directly above a queen-size bed hung a carmine-colored plastic Japanese lantern with a dim red bulb inside. At the head of the bed, glued to the wall, was a large mosaic of small mirrors; on the ceiling above, the same. "Yes!" I cried, "I've been waiting forty-three years for this!" and flopped down on the bed to get the full romantic effect. Unfortunately, however, the ceiling above the mirrors was uneven, and the mirrors imperfectly applied; so the effect was instead hilarious—sort of an animated *Nude Descending a Staircase*. Someone much younger than I—say, forty-three years younger—might have been able to overcome the weirdness; but not me. And several hours later, Mother, just as she had forty-three years earlier on our one-day honeymoon, called from the other room, "Nothing doing! I'm not coming in there till that light is out!"

That was the first evening of our annual wedding

anniversary trip; this is the last. We almost always go to Canada. We were planning this year to spend a couple of days in Sorel, exploring the 103 islands in the St. Lawrence River there. But our usual dog-friendly motel had closed because of labor problems and this, our only other choice, was clearly intended for one-night stands only. So we decided to skip the islands for this year, head east on Sunday morning, and look for a church we'd heard about in a series of e-mails. And after that, *aller ou le vent nous pousse*—to go where the wind pushes us—but in the direction of Quebec City.

So we drove east Sunday morning on the road I presumed ran along the river. It did. But we hadn't quite skipped the islands, after all. The road ran closer and closer to the water, crossed several small inlets, and came finally to a dead end on a swamp maple–choked islet lined with tiny summer camps and docks with duck-hunting boats. I executed probably the tenth of the dozens of U-turns I was to make during this trip and headed back upriver.

RESTAURANT CHEZ GRILL (BABALOU), read the sign on a white building by a bridge. A few cars stood in the parking lot. "Let's have breakfast here," said Mother. We went in. Three long tables ran the length of the single large room, with a kitchen at one end and some rock band instruments at the other. A gaggle of Canadians at the head of the middle table were having a great time. A single elderly man sat at the next. We sat across from him. *"Bonjour."*

It was one of those rare finds: like when a farm boy picks up a rock to toss at a slow-moving cow and discovers the rock is full of silver ore. A great place! It was closing for the winter that afternoon, and Babalou and his wife would head for Florida within the week. We had a pleasant—if somewhat difficult—conversation with the old guy. Mother had eggs and toast and some other stuff, and I had a Kit Babalou: two eggs over easy, homemade toast; *saucisse* (like spicy hotdogs), *baloné* (fried bologna), lettuce and tomato slices, baked beans, and coffee. For the two of us, the bill came to $10.58 Canadian, or $6.67 U.S.

Things kept getting better. After we found the right road, we drove to the St. Francis River Valley and explored both sides down to the mouth, where there's a beautiful little fishing and waterfowl-hunting village, St. Pierreville. You can buy fresh smoked fish or duck at half a dozen smokehouses. Then back up to Odanak, the Indian village that was attacked by Rogers' Rangers in the fall of 1759 during the French and Indian War. Odanak, now an Abenaki First Nation reserve, is a tiny island of English-speaking natives in a sea of French culture, with an Anglican mission church built in 1866. In the yard stands a granite stone with a bronze plaque: *The Reverend Peter Paul Wzokhilan entered Dartmouth College circa 1814. In 1830 he returned as the first Abenaki missionary and teacher to his people . . . author of Indian sermons . . . and hymns . . . translator . . . sponsored as missionary by the Board of Missions, Congregational House, Boston.*

Small world. Small church, too. Only five parishioners besides the priest and us. No piano. The priest, Louis-Marie Gallant, led the hymns a cappella with a booming voice, welcomed the guests from their sister diocese, and preached without notes the best sermon either of us had ever heard on the story of the Pharisee and the tax collector. Probably the high point of the trip.

It's another world: so different from New England. We had supper in Lévis with friends whose living room window looked directly across the river at the incredible lights of Quebec and a huge cruise ship at the city pier. Days Inn let us stay there with our dog, but put us in the cellar. Then east again, downriver, to the cathedral Shrine of Ste.-Anne-de-Beaupré, its narthex and nave lined with discarded crutches, and the Manoir Richelieu, an immense stone hotel and casino recently restored by a new owner. The dog was an extra $25 Canadian, but it was worth it to watch her padding coolly at our heels through the grand hall and salons. The room cost so much we hated to go to sleep, but the full moon reflected on the never-quiet tides of the lower river, and the waves on the rocks were an irresistible soporific.

Next morning, off again: across the river and through the hinterlands to the lovely Manoir Hovey, which is where I'm writing this, with Mother reading in a big chair and the dog snoozing by the fireplace. Neither of them notices I'm preoccupied, though there must be a slight smile on my face. I'm wondering what kind of glue it takes to stick mirrors securely onto ceilings . . .

Money
&
Sex

The Yin of Spring

I'VE NOTICED THE PAST FEW DAYS, down in the village, that people aren't looking each other in the eye. This is quite unusual, since strong eye contact is a normal part of New England communication. But from the post office and the village store to the coffee shop and even the job, people seem to be avoiding conversation.

I shouldn't be surprised; it happens every spring. It's the yin and yang of April.

The robins are back, as amorous and noisy as ever. The redwings are *chir*ring in the swamps. I saw a lone killdeer the other day, fluttering above the mud in Bob Adams's ox pasture. That's the yang: the positive, warm, bright, driving, optimistic force that through the green fuse drives the flower.

The yin is sitting in piles on the dining room table: receipts; a twenty-page questionnaire; inscrutable government forms with mysterious names like 1099 and Schedule C and instructions that defy comprehension. Mother and I are speaking to each other only in defensive terms. Also on the table, she's left copies of various women's magazine, all ominously open to the same regular feature—"Can This Marriage Be Saved?"

It's tax time. The fly in the ointment of spring, the

blight on the early-blooming rose, the bloodthirsty mosquito whining in the ear of joy. Like death, it comes to us all; and like death, it finds some of us ready, and most of us not.

That's the reason for the averted gazes everywhere. Those smart alecks who did their taxes weeks and months ago want to brag to everybody else, like the guy in the TV ad who's lowered his cholesterol and wants to tell the world. Some of those clowns, the ones who filed online, have even gotten their tax refunds back already. They're running around looking for opportunities to tell the rest of us. But those of us who aren't ready will be damned if we'll give 'em a chance to get started. We just look over their shoulders at something behind them whenever they take a breath as if to speak. Misery may love company, but not theirs, by god!

It's not that we mind all that much paying taxes in the first place. They're a necessary part of living in organized society and have been for thousands of years—as necessary (and as much fun) as going to the dentist, changing the oil, and worming the dog. And my reading tells me that income taxes in America are much lower than in many other countries.

On the other hand, I think it's very poor public relations for the president to be videotaped anywhere near tax time tooling from place to place in a fleet of shiny limousines. Ten thirty-foot Cadillacs to get, essentially, one man from here to there? Seems absurd. We could do it a whole lot less expensively in a couple of Cavaliers. And if he trades in Air Force One for another newer model before I can scrape enough together to trade pickups, I'm really going to be some upset!

More or less unfairly, the bogeyman in all of this is the Internal Revenue Service. It's the handiest place to lay the blame for our pain. Granted, they may have some coming—especially for their indecipherable directions—but it's mostly a case of shooting the messenger. They're just doing their job, and in spite of the horror stories we've heard, they do it quite thoughtfully and well.

About twenty years ago I fell afoul of these grim reapers of the public obligation—nothing to do with unpaid taxes, but with unremitted withholding taxes, apparently an even more grievous omission. After several unsuccessful attempts to restructure and collect the debt, they finally sent a very pleasant young man to see us early one spring morning. First, armed with levies, he had gone to our bank and cleaned out our accounts, including our fifteen-year-old daughter's. Then he came to see us at home.

(The breakfast hour, by the way, is when Mafia enforcers also show up. I think both they and the IRS got the idea from the American Indians, who favored dawn for their surprise raids.)

I'd already gone to work. Mother met him at the door in her bathrobe. He showed his ID, suggested that time had run out, and announced an imminent auction of our home, to be held in the front yard. After that pleasant opening gambit, he asked if he might come in. It was a cold morning.

"Nothing doing!" swore Mother, wrapping her robe more tightly about her. "I don't want you looking at my furniture!"

She called me at work, and I came home. It turned into quite a day. After painting vivid pictures of a grisly and inevitable doom that would have done credit to a West Virginia evangelist, and reducing me to a shuddering mass of desperate Jell-O, he gave me just a tiny glimpse of a light at the end of my tunnel. A year or so later I asked him, "Do you guys take sort of a reverse Dale Carnegie course to learn to scare people's pants off like that?"

Yes, he admitted, they did, sort of. By that time, what with his regular visits, genuinely valuable help, and apparent earnest desire to see us out of our difficulty, we'd gotten to be pretty good pals. And for a couple of years afterward, he and his wife and kids stopped in to see us (in the new house—the bank got the old one) when they were staying nearby on vacation.

I think of him now and then, but most often in mid-April, when with grim amusement I remember what a genuinely nice guy he was—and how very little I want to make eye contact with him ever again.

Doin' the Twitch

ONE OF THE MOST DELIGHTFUL THINGS about being married is the constant element of surprise. Every time you think things have settled into the groove you think you'll be in for the rest of your lives, along comes something new: a talent or an idea or a facet of personality that till then had lain dormant, undiscovered, or unrealized. The relationship you had considered stabilized (or stagnant) suddenly takes on a new aspect. Your kids would never believe it, if you told them—might, in fact, even feel threatened by it—but it's true, just the same.

Mother and I a few years ago visited one of those ethnic celebrations in southern New Hampshire, and she surprised the daylights out of me. We were sitting at a little sidewalk café table watching the various dancers and musicians. My hand happened to be resting lightly on her wrist.

The music shifted to an oriental minor key. A troupe of Greek-American men, clad in black-and-white costumes, glided out of a doorway and began one of those sinuous Greek line dances with a big swoop and a quick reverse at the end of each phrase of music. I had to admit they were pretty good— though I've always preferred Polish polkas and Swedish hambos myself.

Then I noticed, quite by chance, that Mother's pulse was picking up. Surreptitiously, I glanced at my watch and checked it—108. I looked sideways at her face. Her nostrils flared ever so slightly, she was breathing visibly, and she twitched! Mother? Twitching? And every time the leader of the dancers glided by—an olive-complected, silver-maned character about seventy years old and at least forty pounds overweight—her pulse quickened to 120.

When the dance was over, she turned toward me with a private little smile on her face, and so help me! there were stars in her eyes! "You know what I'd like to do someday before we're too old?" she asked huskily. "I'd like to go to Greece for a few weeks. Not to the cities, but out in the sticks. I'd like to sit in a sidewalk café and drink ouzo and then get up and dance till I couldn't even walk."

"Well, that'd be nice, wouldn't it?" I agreed. But I didn't mean it, and if she hadn't been in such a state, she'd have picked it up. What I really meant was it'd be nice to be able to afford it, a situation not likely to occur. And what I was thinking was, "If she twitches right here in the streets of Manchester, what outrages might occur on the cobblestones of Kivostos? I think we'd better stick to the refrigerated hills of Etna, New Hampshire."

Yessir, it was quite a surprise, and a shock to my system, after all these years. But the more I thought about it, the more I had to agree it was only fair. After all, I'd been concealing a secret passion myself for some years, not daring to reveal it. Nor was I likely to. First, I felt a little guilty about it; second, the chance to indulge it was about as remote as our taking a tour of the Aegean so that Mother could writhe in the streets of Greek villages.

But—by golly!—last week, as I was going through the advertising section of the newspaper, there it was! And not very far away, either: about seven miles over Hardy Hill, right in Enfield.

The opportunity had to be carefully handled—rather like playing a six-pound fish on two-pound line. Using existing momentum, I diverted it slightly. "Say," I said that night at supper, "instead of just going out to eat this Friday night, why don't we go over to Carole's in Enfield on Saturday? I hear they've got a country-and-western band. Remember how we used to love going to those places and doing the two-step when we were first married?"

She went for it. On Saturday evening at nine we pulled into the parking lot at Carole's. It was jammed with seven-year-old cars and pickup trucks. "My, it's crowded!" observed Mother. "Must be good food."

"Eyah," I said. "Must be."

We found our way into the downstairs bar, a low-ceilinged room filled with noise, smoke, and a lot of very husky people. A bouncer with a black eye collected the cover charge and pointed to the only open table, a circle about the size of a basketball hoop atop a pedestal. We sat and looked around. Shortly, a waitress fought her way to our side and took our drink order.

As we got settled a little, I noticed the music: hard rock. Uh-oh! Wrong night—for country music, anyway. Mother, of course, picked up on it right away, too. "You mean to tell me," she demanded, "that you dragged me out here to listen to rock music?"

"Well, no . . . " I answered, as innocently as possible. "There's something else. Kind of a surprise. It starts at ten o'clock."

The idea of two surprises in one evening didn't seem to do much for her. But she settled down to wait, if a little grumpily. It was too noisy to talk, so we just sat and watched people. Two of them relieved our tedium a few moments later, when one of them, right behind her, smacked the other one a smart one right on the button. The smackee flew backwards just like a movie stunt man, taking out a table and leaving its two occupants still sitting there knee-to-knee, facing each other. Mother leaped to her feet, upsetting our table, as well.

"Sit down! Sit down!" I cried—advice I had learned to credit, the hard way, some years before. But no soap; she was going to get into it for sure. So through the rising hubbub, and before the bouncer arrived, carving his way through the crowd, I shouted, "You've dropped your purse!" That did it; on our hands and knees we went hunting for it on the wet, noisome floor while other strong hands removed the combatants to a cooler place. We resumed our seats, and the waitress brought us another round, on the house.

A little after ten and just before the end of our endurance, the band leader announced a break. Then he added, "Don't go 'way now. We've got dancing girls for you tonight. And the first will be—LAYLA!" I could feel a pair of steel-blue eyes boring into the side of my head, but I was too busy watching the band file off the stage to turn and face them.

Middle-Eastern music began to quaver from the

speakers. The crowd sat hushed and expectant. Suddenly Layla (in real life Carole, the proprietor of the establishment) undulated onto the dance floor. "Well," muttered Mother dryly, "this is a surprise, all right."

Belly dancing (or oriental dancing, as its practitioners apparently prefer to call it) is allegedly one of the world's oldest art forms. It is supposed to have originated in ceremonies surrounding the worship of the earliest deities, which were often female fertility figures. Thus its movements simulate not only the obvious, but the movements of labor, as well— though not the type of labor movement associated with Samuel Gompers and Walter Reuther. So I watched the performance with the detached, objective eye of an aficionado as Layla was succeeded by a lively young lady named "Linda from Boston."

Suddenly I noticed Mother's fingertips resting on my wrist. She was looking at her watch.

Much later, as my little truck chugged back up over the shoulder of Hardy Hill in the moonlight, I hummed happily along with the radio. "You know what?" I said. "Someday, when we finally go to Greece, we ought to take a little swing through Egypt while we're over there. I've always wanted to see the Great Pyramids and the Sphinx."

"Uh-huh," murmured Mother. Then, "Will you please stop that?"

"What? The humming?"

"No," she said. "The twitching!"

The Shack

My construction business had a pretty good run for about ten years, but by 1981 it was pretty clear it wasn't going to make it. The leaks were getting ahead of the pumps. The next four years of our lives were about the worst we've ever had, mostly because there wasn't anything we could do about it. When the end came, in the spring of 1985, we lost just about everything we had: our house, trucks, and equipment. The pain of such abject failure was pretty intense.

The only bright spots were the friends who stood by us, cheered us up, and helped us move our furniture to a warehouse that another friend had lent us. A contractor in the Adirondacks, still another friend, paid off the IRS lien on my equipment for one-sixth the amount of the lien and sold the stuff back to me for $100 a month. Anything he wants—ever!—if I've got it to give, it's his.

At that point we had no more debts, or mortgage payments, and we still had lots of work. In fact, we'd never had more disposable income than in that awful summer. But we had no home or land to build on. All we had managed to keep was our furniture, our health, and our marriage. Quite providentially, we did have a chunk of cash, an insurance settlement

Mother had received for an accident claim. And it really was cash. Stung by several levies on our bank accounts a few months earlier, we kept almost everything in bills. Mother had buried her settlement in the back yard under a cross lettered, "Here lies Puff." Not even an IRS agent, she reasoned, would dig up a dead cat. I'm not so sure that's true.

Again providentially, I stumbled upon a ten-acre plot of woods that had been for sale for a while. The price matched almost exactly what we had. I'll never forget the look on the real estate agent's face when Mother, sitting in his office, began pulling hot, moist one hundred-dollar bills out of her bra. Then, while she began negotiations for a construction loan, I started cutting the long driveway through the woods, across a brook, and up a hill to the site of our next house.

It was at the point, by the way, during the tugs of war with creditors, the IRS, and banks, that Mother took over the management of our finances. She's far better at it than I ever was. I inherited my father's instinct for bookkeeping and careful records, but little creativity in the management of money. So much for the gender-specific roles that were so much a part of our growing up. I don't miss them at all.

The question before us was where to live while I built the house. We could rent, but that would be at least $1,000 a month; not a very attractive option. Since I was the one who'd caused all the pain and trouble, I wasn't in a position to suggest anything difficult. I didn't need to; Mother suggested we camp on our new land while we built the new house. She bought a small, beat-up old trailer for her and our daughter, and I set up a tent to shelter me and my tools.

The trailer was awful. Afraid to light the propane heater, the ladies lived in a virtual tin can with condensation all over the inside of the walls, and dressed each morning in soggy clothes. Life in the tent wasn't much better, but with November approaching, it was about to get much worse. We decided to build a little shack for the three of us, a few dozen feet from the new house. It would cut our costs, and I wouldn't have to drive to my work.

November 5, 1985—Raining steadily, and warm. Moved the girls from the trailer into the shack yesterday. We'll be there till the new house is habitable. Only twelve by twenty feet, and no running water, but I think we can make it for a few months. Martha's room is the loft, up among the rafters like Abraham Lincoln, with about sixty square feet of floor space. Last night , as we were settling down to go to sleep (Mother and I have our mattress on the downstairs floor), Martha stuck her head over the edge of the loft—she looked just like a little blond-ponytailed bat hanging from a barn rafter—and said, very seriously, "Hey, you guys. I can hear everything up here. Don't do anything weird, okay?"

It wasn't a bad job, that shack, if I do say so myself: just barely big enough, with a square-pitch roof that left room for a sleeping and study loft for our daughter. Friends stopped by to help me carry lumber and put it together. It never did get siding outside or drywall inside, but the walls were pretty well insulated. There was electricity for lights, refrigerator, microwave, and typewriter. No running water; I brought six gallons home from town every day, and we used an old-fashioned white porcelain kitchen sink cabinet for washing and cooking. The sink drain was a bucket beneath the tailpiece. No bathroom. The ladies used a camping Porta-Potty while I stood discreetly outside; I used the woods. We took showers at the Dartmouth gym or at friends' houses. Laundry at the Laundromat. Telephone outside on a post about fifty feet away.

Many erstwhile friends disappeared; I think they thought what we had might be contagious. We let 'em go. But we'll never forget the ones who stopped by with best wishes or help. The priest came at least once a week, listened, sympathized, prayed with us. Others braved the primitive conditions to come for supper and seemed to enjoy it.

Saturday, January 4, 1986—Beautiful clear day, cold, but sun-warm in the afternoon. Clouded over thickly now, looks like more snow coming. Garrison Keillor is just reading the week's news from Lake Wobegon. The house is coming along, but slowly. I got black paper onto the part of the roof that's up so far. Somehow, I've got to get the bathroom in before Mother succumbs to terminal depression.

I didn't know it at the time, but it would be a lot longer than I thought before she got her bathroom. If we'd known, I don't know what we might have done. I'm glad we didn't. I had some help now and then, and I still had my tools, but the loft and second floor and the rafters took weeks. The high peak of the living room was three stories above the floor. I cut each rafter, stood it up against the tower of scaffolding, climbed up, and lifted the rafter into place. With the top tacked and tied, I climbed down and nailed the foot of the rafter. Then back up again to nail the top. There were a lot of rafters! The ladies helped wherever they could, but getting off the ground wasn't part of their contract. I think, too, that Mother sensed I needed to work out the shame I felt at putting them through all that. In spite of her own discomfort, she was wonderful to me. As a kid she'd occasionally lived this way, and the fact of it didn't seem to bother her much. It bothered me a lot.

January 5, 1986—More snow, over half a foot, nice and fluffy. My poor new house and piles of lumber were hidden under deep drifts. Shoveled it off this afternoon, feeling kind of blue. If it snows much more before I get the rest of the roof on, the snowbanks are going to be higher than the deck, and I'll be shoveling it uphill. Took a shower at the gym, watched the end of the Patriots game here in the shack, and went to bed just to be unconscious of the whole mess.

A couple of years later, on my way back home from a late-afternoon walk in the woods, I paused beside the now-uninhabited shack and recalled that long, cold winter. The shape of the little building loomed dark and cold against the clouds. A few dozen feet beyond it, the lights of our large but still-unfinished house gleamed warmly. On an impulse, I pushed open the shack door and went in, my head-lamp lighting objects in the gloom—skis in the rafters, an old Bruce Springsteen poster hanging from the loft ceiling, boxes of books, our old foam mattress leaned up against the wall. And even in the cold, the unique aroma of the place, not unpleasant except by association. After almost two years, just stepping into the place was a very emotional experience.

January 14—Pretty cold today. Don't think it got much above ten degrees. Bitter cold outside right now; feels as though it may go to thirty below tonight. Tried to put sheathing on the house this afternoon, but had to stop after every six or seven nails to warm up my left hand, so gave it up as a poor use of time and came in early. Cooked myself up a fancy Chicken Kiev dinner in the microwave. The girls are out visiting, taking showers, and doing laundry. If they're smart, they'll stay as late as they can. It's just a little brisk in here. The kerosene heater warms things up in good shape, but the fumes are fierce.

When we were first married, Mother and I didn't have a washing machine, so we made a weekly run to the nearest coin laundry, in Lake Placid. Both of us remember being put off by some of the other patrons of the place—starch-fed families with beat-up old trucks, grubby kids, and loud voices—who brought great plastic bags and baskets of clothes to wash. We recall feeling that the least they could have done was wash the kids up a little before coming out in public.

No more. Living in the waterless, stoveless shack, we appreciated for the first time how much energy it takes, lacking conveniences that most of us take for

granted, just to survive emotionally and physically—
let alone do it with any style.

If we'd had nothing else to do, it wouldn't have
been too difficult. But we had to maintain our regular jobs in the "normal" world. It's surprising how
hard that is to do without water or a bathroom.

*May 2—After a week of spring—one day almost
eighty—winter has returned. Cold, windy, gray day.
But—hallelujah!—we got the hot water heater hooked
up over in the cellar of the house, and I had my first shower. Never mind it was only forty-four degrees in the
bathroom and there were only three walls. It seemed
heavenly. I wept a little when the hot water came out.*

Sitting there in the cold darkness of the shack,
reminiscing, my breath a cloud in the beam of the
headlamp, I thought of my beans in the oven down
in the kitchen. I clumped down to the warmth of the
house. Then later, when Mother came home, I said,
"You know, just to keep from forgetting how much
we have to be thankful for, we ought to spend a night
or two up in the shack once in a while."

I shouldn't have been surprised that it wasn't anything she wanted to commemorate, let alone reprise.
She was right, too. Now that twenty years have
passed, the pain has abated. But we don't need to be
reminded how much we have to be thankful for. We
think of it every day.

What Killed the Drive-in Movie

IT'S ONE O'CLOCK IN THE MORNING. Mother and I are caught in a time warp. On top of that, we're in dire peril.

You remember the scene in *Dances with Wolves* where Kevin Costner is helping out with the buffalo hunt, and the buffaloes are stampeding all around him? Well, pretend you're there with him, surrounded by the thundering herd, but it's dark and foggy, too, and you can't see. That's what it's like right here right now. Everybody's headed for the exit at once, and I can't see anything through the windshield, and we're right in the middle of the herd, so we can't just pull over and stop. I'm just praying we get out of here in one piece. We've got to usher in church tomorrow.

I'm beginning to appreciate how Adam felt, his last day in the Garden of Eden: This is all Mother's fault.

A couple of days ago, anticipating a weekend at home for a change, the resident cruise director came up with the idea of a little trip down memory lane. "The drive-in movie," she announced, in a burst of rhetoric quite unlike her, "has all but vanished from America. But there's one left in Fairlee, Vermont. Let's go up Saturday night."

"Aw, I dunno. What's playing?"

III

"What's playing?" She looked at me with a bemused expression. "I've never heard you ask that before. Since when has that made a difference?"

"Well, actually, since about forty years ago. I mean, geez, you know . . . "

During our heyday, back in the fifties, asking a girl to go to the movies with you was an invitation to: 1. go to a movie; 2. sit downstairs and maybe hold hands; or 3. sit in the balcony and neck. The nuances of conversation and body language by which the two of you decided which it was going to be were at once wonderful and agonizing.

An invitation to go to the drive-in, however, was quite different. It was practically an explicit invitation to mess around. Not that there weren't some nuances here, too. Nobody in his right mind, for example, would have asked a girl to a drive-in to see *The Ten Commandments*. You want Charlton Heston glowering at you through the windshield? Not likely.

No, you looked for a horror movie, which provided a sort of matrix for comforting each other; or an Annette Funicello / Frankie Avalon beach blanket epic, in which everyone ran around in skimpy suits and eventually fell in love. How could they help it? There was a third alternative: a movie so awful and utterly devoid of interest that nobody bothered to watch it for more than a few minutes—especially with other diversions so near at hand.

It turned out that messing around was not what Mother had in mind this time. She wanted to celebrate the impending end of an era. "I just think we ought to go to one while there's still one to go to," she said, "before they disappear forever. We haven't been to one since the kids were real little, sleeping in the back seat."

So we drove up here just about dusk in the Subaru, which is a far cry from my old man's '57 Chevy or my '46 Plymouth. We brought Cokes and popcorn, and we still had a kid in the back seat—the dog. We hit the previews right on the button, found a place not too far from the exit (I haven't forgotten everything I ever knew), and settled down to watch.

What a flood of memories! Pulling up to the speaker stand and lowering a window to hang the speaker inside the car—while making a mental note not to do the stupidest thing you can do at a drive-in, which is pull out with the speaker still hanging there. Remembering that the little slit at the top of that window is leaking carbon dioxide from your breath into the outside air and attracting mosquitoes. Recalling the choking fumes of the green, smoking mosquito coils we used to light on the dash.

We used bug repellent in a plastic pump bottle, which imparted an interesting, stinging zest to the popcorn. Beside us, a pickup truck was parked backwards, its occupants in lawn chairs in the truck bed. Ahead of us sat a moviegoer who for some reason kept pumping his brake pedal nervously, till some guy walked over to his car and asked him to cut it out.

I don't know where she learned it, but the dog in the back seat was doing a perfect imitation of the kids, which prompted me to do an imitation of myself as a young father: "Hey! Settle down back there!" At least there was only one of her, so there wasn't anyone for her to pinch.

The night was cool, and there were three sets of lungs going in the car. Right away the windshield began to fog up. "You got a towel?" I asked. She had, and I used it; but it was all greasy with popcorn butter and didn't improve things at all. What a mess! Cursing, I reached for my handkerchief. Thirty years ago I would have said, "Oh, well . . . "

Somehow the Fairlee Drive-in has managed to preserve, more or less intact, a genuine 1950s intermission film, featuring footage of uncomfortably dressed kids with slicked-down hair eating hotdogs and ice cream cones, and the notices of how many minutes are left before the start of the second feature. "Visit our refreshment stand!" it urges. Did kids like that ever really exist, with those vapid grins? My old yearbooks affirm they did.

During the second feature the nostalgia finally began to get the better of me. I sat up straighter, reached my right arm around Mother's shoulders, and hugged her a little. She does have pretty good ideas, I thought, and I'm awfully glad I was one of 'em.

But within two minutes my right deltoids were in spasm, and my hand was falling asleep. A sore spot also was developing on the outside of my right thigh, where it was pressed against the shift lever. End of romance. "You know what killed the drive-ins?" I asked, rubbing my shoulder. "Bucket seats and four on the floor."

Economics 101

"MOM AND DAD? LACROSSE STARTS next week, and I'm going to need a new stick."

It's probably only a coincidence that lacrosse season and the need for new equipment occur just about the time income taxes are due. But the coincidence couldn't be more painful even if it had been dreamed up by some sadistic genius.

"Can I have some money for the movies? Fifteen dollars ought to be enough. Or if you don't have the cash, maybe I could take the ATM card."

Clothes. School lunches. A trip to Montreal with the French class. Always something. Having an active kid in school can be the death of a thousand cuts for what is laughingly called your "disposable income." Yet you hate to turn 'em down. There they are, up to their ears in new experiences, exploring new avenues of expression, and on the verge of everything; and what if your stinginess were to blight their young lives?

Our first two kids were two years apart, and I don't recall having gone through too much of that with them. Good thing; there weren't too many disposable family resources available when they were in adolescence. But the third kid was seven years behind the second, so in effect she was an only child:

a princess with exclusive rights to a bathroom built for three, transported everywhere by two chauffeurs devoted to her personal transportation needs, and sensing that we were eager to give her—in our last chance as parents—all the opportunities once shared by the three of them.

But it wasn't just money that was the problem. It was the constant tug of war between what she felt she needed and what we felt were reasonable limits. This leads, in virtually every family, to the same old arguments several times a week: Why can't I? Everybody else in my class is going to! These sneakers don't fit anymore! They're stunting my feet. Every one of my friends has television in her room—cable! If I had my own computer, I could do my reports even on nights when Dad is working on his. The objects change, but the arguments are as old as Socrates. We've all heard 'em. Hell, we all used 'em ourselves!

Most parents respond to them, as we did, with an allowance, which is intended to provide for the child's small needs and pleasures and promote "responsible use of money." And it does, sort of. But then there are constant off-budget items, like a new jacket or skis or school lunches; and almost every one of these items is the occasion of another tearful confrontation. It became clear that there had to be a better way to tackle the problem.

Mother came up with it. "Look," she said to our daughter one day. "Do you suppose you could sit down and make out a list of everything you spend money on in the course of a year? I mean everything. You make out the list; we'll go over it together to see if it's realistic; and then we'll make out a budget. It's got to include savings and charitable donations, by the way. Then we'll divide the total amount by fifty-two, and the result is what I'll give you every week—if, and only if, and only after you've accounted for every penny spent the previous week.

"You can borrow occasionally from one part of the budget to pay for something else—say, from clothes to pay for entertainment—but that money's got to be paid back. Every so often we'll take a look at how it's going, to see if it needs adjusting. What do you think?"

Well, that was the easy part, at least by comparison. It was still in the conceptual stage, and the disagreements were mild. They produced a budget, and the weekly amount came to $25, a figure that surprised us all. But a deal was a deal, and Mother made the first disbursement.

The hard part came at the end of each week, when the accounts were presented in order to trigger the next installment. Friday was payday, so the discussions occurred Thursday evening. Memory proved a poor tool in reconstructing the week's financial activities, and "about twelve dollars" didn't cut it as an accurate expense figure. The disagreements were lengthy and loud—rather like a Moroccan bazaar. I began to find Thursday evening a great time to go to the gym.

But, by golly, it worked! The accounts became lucid and reliable, and the kid began to enjoy the administration of her funds. The sweater or blouse that in the past she'd let her mother buy her off-budget, she now found too expensive. She had money in the bank and put her own money into the plate at church. She began to lobby for her check Thursday evening instead of Friday; by depositing it on the way to school, before the weekend, she could make a few cents more interest.

After college as a sports medicine major, she looked for a job in physical rehabilitation. But she needed another degree to go anywhere with it, so she gravitated instead to the business office of a rehab clinic. It was a natural fit. Health maintenance organizations pay millions in benefits for rehabilitation services prescribed by doctors. But they do not often pay them willingly, and someone at the clinic has to get on the phone and jawbone over the details of coverage as described in the policies. The kid found that her clinic was losing a lot of money by losing these arguments or considering them too much trouble to pursue. And she also found her niche, her métier! I often smile at the thought of what those telephone conversations must sound like, and wonder if the guys at the HMOs take off for the gym when they hear her voice, the way I used to.

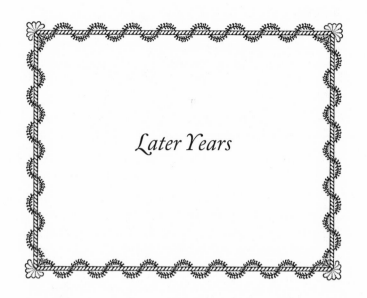

Later Years

The Dining Room Plywood

It's Christmas night, almost midnight. The last of the dinner guests and cheery good wishes have faded into the darkness. Fresh snow whispers at the skylight behind my head. The dishwasher purrs away at one load of dishes, while another awaits admission.

The cat prowls quietly among the exotic aromas of the new gifts under the tree. The dog, worn out with keeping an eye on nine dinner plates and their nine proprietors all at once, is slumped in a heap at the foot of the bed, and Mother is chatting on the phone with one of our kids on the West Coast. I've finished off all the unhealthful and sinful treats that were in my stocking and am just beginning to eye the disciplinary ones: sugar-free, no salt, low-fat.

I can't help but reflect, listening to the dishwasher at work, that Mother and I have kept the tradition alive: that we've been entertaining for over forty years without ever owning a dining room table.

When we were first married and living in our leaky, ten-dollar-a-month apartment, our entire suite of furniture was given to us by sympathetic villagers—a single bed (we slept like spoons in a kitchen drawer), a rough board table three feet square, two mismatched and much-painted kitchen chairs, and a three-burner gas range. And of course there was that damned oven door that you had to prop shut with a piece of lath if you wanted to bake.

We didn't mind any of this much because we were young, flexible, in love, and full of high hopes of better things to come. And almost immediately our hopes were rewarded. One neighbor gave us an old double bed; another came by with a wicker easy chair as well as a rustic settle with a back that rotated to the horizontal to form a table fully thirty inches by four feet. Never mind that nobody with legs longer than twenty inches could sit at it comfortably. We were on our way!

This evening, over forty years later, we and our guests—nine of us in all—sat at that same table, miraculously expanded to four feet by eight feet. The tablecloth hung well down on all four sides, so you'd hardly have known that under it was an old piece of plywood much traveled, much altered, and much marked with historic graffiti. King Arthur's round table itself couldn't have given us as much pleasure, or excited more reminiscence, than that old settle table and its top.

Early on, when we were still on the career track, we dined with small groups of colleagues and for those occasions kept on hand a half-sheet of plywood, its corners slightly rounded, to slap onto the old settle as a tabletop. Mother and I sat on the ends, where our knees bumped the base, and the guests in relative comfort on the sides. The high point during this stage of our lives was the evening we entertained my principal and his wife. Mother was nervous to the point of distraction, but the food and the ambiance were flawless. Then, as she prepared to clear for dessert, she suddenly blanked on whether to take away right or left. So she nodded to me, and we lifted up the plywood top—cloth, dishes, and all—and carried it into the kitchen, leaving our principal and his wife sitting facing each other across the old settle in the dining room. We set the dessert and coffee on, brought the whole thing back, and finished dinner. Ah, we were smooth as silk in those days!

Later our dinner parties got larger, so we hauled out our plywood bed board, which added two feet to the length of our table. Between social events, we slid it back under our mattress. But we used it also, without a tablecloth, whenever all three kids were doing their homework at once, and we wanted to keep an eye on them. This was when the graffiti began to appear: *No school today 2/3/82. Ozreal* (an ill-fated cat) *was here. Right now I'm listening to* General Hospital. *Ida and Will slept here.* The piece of plywood, as the kids grew up and left one by one, took on a bawdy, sentimental value far beyond the intrinsic.

In recent years, with guests often numbering twelve and more, we've taken to using card tables grouped in the living room. But this morning, just as I was uncoiling from the rigors of Christmas Eve midnight Eucharist and the early gift-swapping, and beginning to think about a brisk walk and a nice nap, Mother sprang her latest. Did I have a full sheet of plywood in the shop? No. Did I have a smaller piece, say, two by four feet? Well, yes . . . Good! Cut this old tabletop in half and stick the small piece in the middle, cut it into a slight oval, and we'll have an eight-foot tabletop. And you'd better put some cleats on the bottom so it won't slide around.

Holy Toledo! If her husband were a surgeon, would she casually ask him to remove her appendix before going out for the newspaper? Yes, I think she would.

A couple of hours later, surrounded by a pile of tools—saws, drill, screwdriver, clamps, straightedge, router, biscuit joiner, belt sander, laminate trimmer, and Rolaids—I was done. I skidded the monster up the cellar stairs, and she helped me set it down over the old settle. We covered it with a couple of cloths, and you couldn't have told, without lifting its skirts and peeking, that it wasn't a perfectly normal dining room table.

It is a little tippy, though, so Mother and I, by tacit agreement, grasp it firmly, each at his end, whenever a guest makes to rise or plants his elbows on it at his place.

One of these days, we keep telling ourselves, we're going to have a real table. But I don't know. What would we do then with this old beauty? Hang it on the wall like the round table at Camelot? Hmm . . . I wonder if we could get an oval bed eight feet long . . .

Mother's Improbable Odyssey

CHURCH SERVICE WAS OVER. I WAS standing innocently on the lawn sipping a paper cup of coffee, when a woman about my age sidled over to me with a quizzical look on her face.

"That stuff you put in the paper," she said. "I can't believe it's all true. Is it all true?"

It occurred to me as odd that a woman who'd just made a public profession in which she affirmed a belief in virgin birth, walking on water, miraculous healing, and corporal resurrection would quibble over, say, a fish I had claimed to have caught or a stranger-than-fiction tale from my unsuccessful career as a bear hunter. I reflected several moments about her question, which soon lost itself in the larger philosophical question, what is Truth?—a vague area in which I am infinitely more comfortable.

Those of us who write a lot wrestle often with the slippery boa constrictor of truth. We know that, even though a certified thermometer may indicate a temperature of, say, sixteen degrees below zero Fahrenheit, it is no less true to exclaim, after sticking your nose out the door, "Wow! It must be ninety below out there!" A lot depends upon the spirit in which a thing is said or written, as well as that in which it is read or heard. The mother of a boyhood friend of

125

mine once said, "When Bill talks about eating a White Tower hamburger, you'd think it was a four-course meal." So in response to the original question: Yes, it's true, every blessed word of it!

But I'm a mere piker and bush-leaguer compared to my wife. Mother's whole life, from infancy onward, has been such an incredible string of Dickensian improbabilities and hairbreadth escapes from calamity that, if she were to write her autobiography, it'd be indexed in the library, alphabetically by author, under "Fiction." The string continues today.

Several months ago, after a visit by our older daughter, Mother drove her to Manchester to catch her plane back to the West Coast. On the way, they talked about a purple sweater our daughter had fancied in a J. Crew catalog. So after dropping her off, Mother thought, hmm, there's a J. Crew outlet right over in Portsmouth. I'll just zip over there and see if they've got it.

Nope, they hadn't. Nuts! But then she thought, well, it's early, and I'm almost in Maine, anyway, and there's a J. Crew in Freeport. I'll go look up there. Nope, still no purple sweater. But the clerk in Freeport suggested that if Mother diverted only slightly from the regular route back to New Hampshire, she could hit the J. Crew in North Conway. It was late in the afternoon by then, so she dropped in on some friends in Brunswick and spent the night there first.

See what I mean? For a purple sweater! And some folks think my life improbable!

Next morning, Mother started over the back roads toward North Conway. Naturally, she got lost, stopped for directions, and before long was threading her way through the bushes over decidedly secondary roads.

An aside: Both Mother and I grew up reading the heroic tales of derring-do in the *Reader's Digest*. You've read them: the mild-mannered dry goods clerk who sees a gasoline truck smash into the pumps and suffers severe burns rescuing the driver from certain immolation; the kid who spots a dog and its owner struggling in a hole in the ice, grabs a ladder, saves them both, and barely survives the rescue himself. Mother still reads those stories. I don't; the *Digest* and I parted company philosophically about twenty-five years ago. But she and I are sure that, should either of us ever stumble across an accident or crisis requiring immediate and heroic action, there'd be no question of our responses, even at imminent peril of death.

So there she was, humming happily through the woods of rural Maine and listening to a radio evangelist. His text happened to be, "Whatever you want or need, ask for it in the name of Jesus Christ!" Just then she spotted a column of smoke rising from a house beside the road ahead. Chimney fire, she thought, and slowed down to look for someone to tell. What she saw was much more spectacular: an attached three-car garage just catching fire, and great gouts of smoke belching out the open bay doors.

She stopped and got out. The only sound was the crackling of the hot, greedy fire. She could feel the heat on her face over one hundred feet away. Just then a man ran from the house and dashed toward the garage. Mother crouched in the ditch beside the road and shouted at him to stop, not to go in there. He shouted back that his 1936 Cadillac was in there. He'd just called the fire department. It turned out later he'd been working on the old classic and dropped his trouble light, which had smashed and ignited gasoline on the garage floor.

The heat was too intense. It stopped him in the driveway, and he collapsed. Here was the exact opportunity for which *Reader's Digest* had been preparing her all these years. But she found that in the event, she couldn't do it. She just didn't dare get any closer to the fire, which had now engulfed the garage. Gasoline and ammunition were exploding inside, cartridges whizzing wildly through the air. The man lay supine on the driveway, twitching as he roasted.

"Roll down the hill!" she shouted; he did. She caught him as he reached her, and he slumped in her arms, his face ashen. So she just held him and waited for help. A fire engine pulled up, with only two volunteers aboard—all that had been available. "Help me!" she hollered. They ran over, took a look, mumbled something about his heart condition, told her she was on her own, and thundered off to tackle the fire. Neighbors began to arrive with doleful comments about inadequate fire insurance and the dog, which was still chained to the smoking doghouse. The poor homeowner began to thrash in Mother's arms, his face livid. An ambulance was coming, somebody said, but nobody knew when.

Then an inspiration struck her, born of her recent radio listening. "Listen!" she said. "Do you go to church?" Yes, he nodded. "Do you believe in Jesus Christ?" He nodded again.

"Then in the name of Jesus," she ordered, "be calm! Lie still!" Amazingly, he did. But suddenly his eyes rolled back in his head, and she thought, "Good Lord! Not that calm!"

A few minutes later the ambulance finally arrived, loaded him in, and disappeared. Meanwhile, the firemen were saving the house and the poor, scorched dog. As things calmed down, Mother remembered North Conway and the sweater.

Well, that was the story she told me when she got home at last—just before I called the state police to see if they had any idea where she might be. I must have registered some incredulity at the tale, because she was at pains to show me the sweater she'd found in North Conway, as well as the ashes still sticking to her van. When a few days later she told me she'd called and learned that the man with the bad heart was doing fine, I made some impolite comment about trying to gild a lily. Privately, I thought, "Boy, Lange! You've told some beauts, but you're out of your league. She's a genius!" And then the Christmas card arrived, with a gift and a photo of the still-breathing old guy in the bushes of Maine.

So don't ever ask. Be calm and lie still. They're true, every word of 'em!

Thank You So Much!

If it isn't written, it doesn't exist. I don't know how many times I've used that line over the past few years. But that's all it is: a line. It's not an expression of principle; for I know that many societies without written languages have kept alive and accurate for centuries the history and lore of their cultures at least as well as we have, for all our meticulous recording. So it's just a line I use to inform my wife that whatever it was she asked me to do last week—or the message she gave me, or the things she asked me to pick up at the grocery store—does not exist anywhere within my responsibilities. It's like whatever you were typing on your word processor, without saving, just before the electricity went off. A vague memory, perhaps, but without power to compel or inform.

    I. A. Package box with note, pup tent, tablecloth, using "popcorn" from Tucker's bed.
    B. Label for Tyler Langes.
    C. Put in van.

Oh, man! She did it! I would have sworn she wouldn't. There went my day of rest.

Thanksgiving is my favorite holiday, both philosophically and logistically. Philosophically because giving thanks is a demonstrably healthful thing to do; logistically because, unlike the other holidays, which add a day to a weekend, Thanksgiving creates a week with two Fridays.

    II. A. Refill Tucker's dog bed with bag of sawdust on
        my office floor.
    B. Put back under table.

It's also always been a holiday on which I've had to do virtually nothing but enjoy life. Ever since my childhood, there's been a female ball of fire in the kitchen—first my grandmother, then my mother, and finally my wife—who set the table with the best silver and china, produced the finest dinner of the year, and washed the dishes and pots and pans afterward. All I had to do was decide whether I wanted gravy on my vegetables, too.

    III. A. Wind up green extension cord.
    B. Put in closet (the one with light bulbs).

In recent years, however, the ball of fire in the kitchen has begun to smolder a bit and exhibit some dissatisfaction with the difference between our levels of activity, especially with eight or ten people coming to dinner. "You enjoy company," she says. "So you help."

Now, I don't mind helping some . . . no, that's not true; I'm willing to help if I can't get out of it. But first I have to exhaust a series of ploys that have worked pretty well for over sixty years.

I begin with the Ill-Tempered Gambit: "Okay, tell

me what you want done; let's get it over with." This
is delivered with arms akimbo or fingers drumming
on a resonant surface. Its purpose is to render dealing
with me more unpleasant than doing the work herself. It worked like a charm with my mother all the
way through adolescence.

IV. Replace dimmer switch in dining room.

Then there's the Klutz Pretense: "Mash what?
Mash the potatoes? Which pot has the potatoes?
What do you want me to do it with—this fork? Just
mash 'em up, hey? I thought maybe you put something into 'em first. How many cups of salt?" This is
designed to make it less trouble for her to do the job
herself than try to instruct me. It worked for decades
but has lately worn thin.

V. Take trash cans and buckets downstairs.

Now I've come up with a new one. "Look," I say,
"I don't mind helping"—it's still not true—"but I do
mind your making it up as you go along. I can't just
stand here all day like a potted palm"—I got that one
from Oliver North's lawyer—"waiting for you to
think up things for me to do. I need you to give me a
list of what you want me to do, so I have some idea of
the number and limits of my responsibilities." She
hates to make lists; I knew she'd never do it.

VI. Retrieve black shelf I slid down your stairs and
    wash with brush and hose. Put in my side of cel-
    lar.

VII. Take skin off cooked squash, bag squash.

Not only did she make a list, but she made it long, and she made it so simple that even I could figure out what she meant. Note the preemption implicit in "bag squash." She knew that if she wrote the obvious—"Take skin off cooked squash and bag it"—I'd employ the old Klutz Pretense and put the skin into the bag.

VIII. Make as much ice as possible. Throw out partially evaporated cubes first.
IX. Water plant on left of living room (facing room with back to stove).
X. Type "General Thanksgiving" in narrow format, very plain font.
XI. Peel onions. Chop onions and celery, crush pecans, rinse Cuisinart.
XII. Make bed.

I scanned the list before starting. Easiest stuff first, or hardest? What would Dale Carnegie do? Henry Ford? Dagwood? Hagar? There was only one job that might not get done if I left it till last—freezing the ice—so I did that first. Then the most complicated: taking the Styrofoam corn out of the dog's bed and using it to pack a Christmas box. Then the quickies that would cut the list down fast to just a few items. Finally I was done, with enough time to take a shower before the guests were due to arrive. I crossed off the last item and put the canceled list on her desk.

This morning I found it on my desk, rolled like a diploma and tied with a piece of gold cord, with a pillow mint inside. I opened it. She'd added another item to the list.

Thank you so much!

Envoi

Well, there it is . . . some of it. There's so much more. We've been married about two-thirds of our lives, after all, and every one of those years has been densely packed. The complete tale would be interesting to nobody but us. These stories and essays are simply reflections. In effect, I'm asking, What is there about this life we've shared that's been so vital? And would I do it again?

The answer to that last question has not always been yes. Because marriage hasn't been for us—perhaps, in fact, isn't for anyone—a walk in the park. We're different: politically, spiritually, emotionally, and physically. We want different things from life. We've experienced deep anger and frustration with each other; we've gone through an anguished separation; and there have been days when I've thought that anything else was better than staying with this lady any longer. On the other hand, if I'm honest, I'll admit she's put up with far more grief than she's ever caused me.

Marriage, I've concluded, is like living in New England: Generally, it's a lovely place to be. But there are days when you wonder why in the world you got into this. Then, when you try to imagine where else you might go, you have to admit there's no place on earth it's likely to be better.

I didn't arrive at that simile after only two or three fracases; it's taken literally hundreds. The result is what's called perspective. I remember how I felt when I made that commitment so long ago and reflect upon all we've endured and enjoyed together since. What could ever replace that? I remember how many arguments I've considered terminal to our relationship, and how the clouds have blown away eventually in every case. And I can see that, as we ourselves gradually slow down with age, we now spend less time than ever clearing our skies. We don't have that much time to waste in anger and recrimination; I regret that I didn't know decades ago there never was that much time.

In all your life, there's no one with whom you'll argue more fiercely than with your spouse, and probably no one who will so frustrate you, because no one can win. When it's over, there you are, living in the same house and sleeping in the same bed (except, perhaps, for a few nights). And the substance of the disagreement remains—even though settled—still an issue.

That describes and demands an implicit compromise, which is what most of a successful marriage is. Gradually you come to realize that before it's over, one of you probably is going to need the other to answer basic physical needs, just as your children needed you when they were tiny and helpless. I have a feeling that's when you truly understand the meaning of marriage—and just in time, too.

Canada geese mate for life. I shall never, as long as I live, forget coming upon a pair of them beside a little river in the Canadian Arctic. They'd been left behind by their south-migrating flock. The goose lay upon the bank, dying. An arctic fox sat on his haunches about fifty yards away, watching with impatient interest. The old gander tried again and again to lift his mate's head with his bill, but she couldn't rise. Suddenly he stopped, raised his head toward the sky, and cried out over and over the full, awful load of his breaking heart. It was terrible to hear. And yet how lucky they had been, till that moment of parting by death, to have shared such a life, and such a love!

About the Author

WILLEM LANGE WAS BORN IN 1935.
A child of deaf missionary parents, he grew up communicating in Sign Language. He first came to New England in 1950 to attend prep school as an alternative to reform school in his native New York State.

Will earned his undergraduate degree from the College of Wooster in Ohio. Between terms, he worked as a ranch hand, Adirondack guide, preacher, construction laborer, bobsled run announcer, assembly line worker, cab driver, bookkeeper, and bartender. From 1962 to 1968, he taught high school English in northern New York and spent summers as an Outward Bound instructor.

From 1968 to 1972 Will directed the Dartmouth Outward Bound Center. Since 1972 he has been a building and remodeling contractor in Hanover, New Hampshire.

In 1973 Will founded the Geriatric Adventure Society, a group of outdoor enthusiasts whose members have traveled much of the world by ski, canoe, and climbing boot.

In 1981 Will began writing his weekly newspaper column, "A Yankee Notebook," for *The Valley News.* He's also a commentator and host for Vermont Public Radio and both Vermont and New Hampshire

Public Television. His annual readings of Charles Dickens's *A Christmas Carol* have been a tradition in the Upper Valley since 1975. Will has published four books and earned an Emmy Award nomination for one of his pieces on Vermont Public Television.

Will and his wife, Ida, met during the summer of 1959 and were married twelve weeks later, after a whirlwind romance. Ida has been the proprietor of a kitchen design business since 1990.

The Langes live on a dead-end dirt road in Etna, New Hampshire. They have three children and—so far—four grandchildren.